Longman English Interactive 4

Activity and Resource Book

Michael Rost

Longman

Longman English Interactive 4
Activity and Resource Book

Acknowledgments
We wish to extend our sincere appreciation to Victoria Badalamenti, Elizabeth Ianotti, Jennifer Benichou, and the students of the English Language Center at LaGuardia Community College for inspiring the concept of this Activity and Resource Book. Additionally, we wish to thank the following users, reviewers, and piloters of *Longman English Interactive* for contributing ideas toward the development of the Activity and Resource Book:

Elizabeth Ianotti, Jennifer Benichou, *LaGuardia Community College*
Banu Yaylali, Kathy Biache, *Miami-Dade Community College*
Alfredo Rodriguez, *KPMG Mexico*
Julie Fanara, *Howard Community College*

The author wishes to thank Kathleen Field, Nancy Blodgett, Lynn Contrucci, Hugo Loyola, Irene Frankel, and Sherry Preiss for their guidance and support during the development of this activity book. The author also wishes to thank the entire Pearson multimedia team for their ongoing development of *Longman English Interactive*.

Pearson Education, 10 Bank Street, White Plains, NY 10606

Cover design: Inez Sovjani
Cover photo: Mark Harmel/Stone (Getty Images)
Text design: Quorum Creative Services
Text composition: TSI Graphics
Illustrations: Kenneth Batelman
Photo credits: **page 14:** GoodShoot/SuperStock; **page 21:** Zoran Milich/Masterfile

---

LONGMAN ON THE **WEB**

Longman.com offers online resources for teachers and students. Access our Companion Websites, our online catalog, and our local offices around the world.

Visit us at **longman.com**.

ISBN: 0-13-152085-7

Printed in the United States of America
1 2 3 4 5 6 7 8 9 10–WC–09 08 07 06 05

Contents

	Scope and Sequence	iv
	To the Teacher	viii
	To the Student	x
	Progress Checks	xvii
A.1	The Straight Story	1
A.2	A Hot Lead	10
A.3	Jackie, the Actress	19
A.4	A Confrontation	27
B.1	Talia's Brilliant Plan	35
B.2	Dean's Double Cross	43
B.3	Another Confession	52
B.4	A Lesson Learned	61
C.1	A Canceled Celebration	69
C.2	Jackie's Big Scene	79
C.3	Hard Evidence	88
C.4	Just Being Honest	98
	Appendix 1: Audioscript	107
	Appendix 2: Vocabulary Terms	115
	Appendix 3: Language Functions	121
	Answer Key	129

Scope and Sequence

Module	Video Listening	Vocabulary	Speaking	Grammar	
A.1 **The Straight Story**	Predict conversation topics; Listen for information about relationships and main events in a story.	Words and their antonyms	Catch up on things; Link back; Change the subject.	• Verb tense review • Negative *yes/no* questions and tag questions • Verb (+ object) + infinitive	
A.2 **A Hot Lead**	Predict people's opinions; Listen for information about events; Understand people's strategies.	Phrases with *line*	Ask about and talk about problems; Suggest and respond to solutions.	• The passive • Quantifiers • Verb + gerund or verb + infinitive	
A.3 **Jackie, the Actress**	Predict conversation topics; Listen for the main purpose and details of people's plans.	Occupations connected to acting	Ask for general and specific impressions; Respond to questions about impressions.	• Present perfect and present perfect continuous • Embedded *wh-* and *yes/no* questions • Participial adjectives	
A.4 **A Confrontation**	Predict how people will interact; Listen to understand people's relationships and their reasons for asking questions.	Expressions with food	End a conversation; Suggest keeping in touch; Confirm the next meeting; Say good-bye.	• Modals of possibility and probability • Reflexive and reciprocal pronouns • Modals of possibility and probability in the past	
B.1 **Talia's Brilliant Plan**	Predict actions; Listen for specific plans and the speaker's main purpose.	Words that describe hair	Give, accept, and downplay compliments.	• *Make, have, get, let,* and *help* • *So* and *neither* • Future time clauses	
B.2 **Dean's Double Cross**	Predict reactions; Listen for details in reported speech and for key statements that show emotions.	Phrases with *keep*	Interrupt someone and ask someone not to interrupt; Express disagreement, skepticism, and sarcasm; Concede.	• Compare: Simple past with *when* and past continuous with *when* • Reported imperatives • Subject adjective clauses	

Task Listening	Pronunciation	Reading	On the Web	Writing
Listen to advertising pitches and choose the picture that matches the description.	• Unstressed words: *a, an, the, and, but* • Vowel sounds in *soon, use,* and *good*	An article about successful international marketing campaigns	Research a popular product and its selling points.	Write a description of a product's selling points.
Listen to guidelines given to new customer service representatives at their job orientation, and put the information in a chart.	• Falling intonation for statements and *wh-* questions • Unstressed words: *is, was*	An article about emotional intelligence	Research successful people.	Write a biography and give your opinion about a successful person's EQ.
Listen to instructions for how to register for classes, and choose places on a campus map.	• Rising intonation for some questions • Stress in noun compounds	An article about why people think cell phones are important	Research cell phones.	Write a descriptive/explanatory paragraph about a cell phone feature.
Listen to callers making restaurant reservations, and enter their information in a reservation book.	• Stress in sentences • Unstressed words: *have*	An article with tips about how to have a successful business lunch	Research restaurants in different cities.	Write a description of a good restaurant for special occasions.
Listen to an excerpt from a documentary about warning signals, and put pictures into the correct categories.	• Linking words (vowel to vowel) • Stress on pronouns in responses	An article about technological gadgets	Research James Bond's spy gadgets.	Write a descriptive paragraph about a gadget.
Listen to a conversation at a restaurant, and put photos in the correct order.	• Stress on pronouns for emphasis or contrast • Non-final intonation	An article about effective relaxation techniques	Research ways of reducing stress.	Write a paragraph comparing ways to relieve stress.

Module	Video Listening	Vocabulary	Speaking	Grammar	
B.3 **Another** **Confession**	Predict conversation topics; Listen for details of recalled information and for the speaker's main intentions.	Expressions related to dating and romance	Remind someone about past events; Comment about memories; Express regret.	• Future conditional • Past perfect • Infinitives after adjectives and nouns	
B.4 **A Lesson** **Learned**	Predict intentions; Listen for sequences of actions and for ideas that show relationships.	Phrases with *clear*	Identify a problem; Suggest a course of action; Respond to a suggested course of action.	• Future in the past • Passive causative • Reported statements	
C.1 **A Canceled** **Celebration**	Predict reactions; Listen for advice and to understand people's personalities.	Words with *over*	Place blame on yourself or someone else; Comfort someone and respond to comforting.	• *Wish* • Past unreal conditional • *Be supposed to*	
C.2 **Jackie's Big** **Scene**	Predict conversation topics; Listen for information in stories and for reasons for people's actions.	Phrasal verbs with *come*	Express enthusiasm; Express reluctance, worry, and apathy; Express sympathy. .	• Present unreal conditional • Past perfect continuous • *Should have*	
C.3 **Hard Evidence**	Predict what will happen next; Listen for the outcome of a situation and for people's plans.	Literal and figurative expressions	Show anger; Calm someone down.	• Future continuous • Object adjective clauses • Passive modals	
C.4 **Just Being** **Honest**	Predict conversation topics; Listen for information about events in people's lives and for ideas about relationships.	Phrases with *break*	Talk about intentions and plans; Wish someone luck; Ask for future updates.	• Adjective clauses: review and expansion • Auxiliary verbs for emphasis • Review of phrasal verbs	

Task Listening	Pronunciation	Reading	On the Web	Writing
Listen to a psychology lecture on memory and take notes.	• Stress in words with *any-, every-, some-,* and *no-* • Rising intonation to ask for clarification	An article about specialty coffees	Research specialty coffees.	Write a descriptive paragraph about a specialty coffee.
Listen to stories on the evening news, and choose the newspaper headline that matches each story.	• Stress in words with prefixes • Voiced *th* sound in *this*	An article about folk tales with an example from ancient China	Research traditional stories.	Retell a traditional story.
Listen to statements, and take a test to find out if you are an optimist or a pessimist.	• Reduced phrases: *supposed to, have to, has to, want to* • Unstressed words: *could, would*	An article about flower-giving customs in different countries	Research how to buy flowers.	Write a paragraph about how to buy flowers.
Listen to an interview with a famous interviewer, and organize the information.	• Reduced phrases: *should have, could have, would have* • Linking words together (changes in sounds)	An article about surveillance technology	Research television shows that are based on videos of real people or animals.	Write paragraph describing a TV show.
Listen to a man talk about a nightmare, and put pictures in the correct order.	• Consonant clusters • Stress in words ending in *-tion* and *-ate*	An article about proverbs in different countries	Research proverbs from different countries.	Write a paragraph comparing 2 proverbs from different cultures.
Listen to speeches given at a party, and match quotes with the correct person.	• Stress in phrasal verbs • Vowels followed by *-r*	An article about movie endings	Research classic films.	Write a summary of reviews of a classic film.

To the Teacher

About *Longman English Interactive*

Longman English Interactive is a comprehensive multimedia course that lets students work at their own pace on a range of language learning activities. *Longman English Interactive 4* consists of software (two CD-ROM disks) that students use in a computer learning lab or on their own computers. Each unit is based on a scene from an ongoing video story, with closely linked exercises for listening, speaking, grammar, pronunciation, vocabulary, and reading development. Each unit of the CD-ROM course provides up to 4 hours of self-paced instruction employing extensive video, audio, and animated graphics, and including interactive exercises, review quizzes, and immediate feedback.

About the *Longman English Interactive Activity and Resource Book*

This *Activity and Resource Book* is designed to serve as a personal or classroom resource for learners and a management tool for teachers and course coordinators who are using the *Longman English Interactive* multimedia software.

- Simple screenshots help students quickly learn how to use the software.
- Progress Checks for each unit enable students to keep a record of completed activities and scores on the review quizzes in the CD-ROM course.
- Additional listening tasks let students review the course audio segments. Each *Activity and Resource Book* includes an audio CD.
- Expanded grammar exercises for each grammar point allow students to consolidate learning.
- Vocabulary reviews offer students new ways of remembering key words and phrases from each unit.
- Language Functions exercises give students additional controlled practice with the functional language expressions from the unit.
- Application Activities provide multiple ways for students to apply what they have learned in realistic ways.

This *Activity and Resource Book* can be used as a self-access learning guide or as a classroom text for students who are using *Longman English Interactive*. Best used after completing each unit of the *Longman English Interactive* CD-ROM course, students can use the *Activity and Resource Book* at home, in the computer lab, or in the classroom. Students can complete each exercise (Listening, Grammar, Vocabulary, and Language Functions) on their own or with a study partner or group and consult the Grammar Explanations at the end of each unit of the *Activity and Resource Book* as needed. They can also refer to the Audioscript, a glossary of vocabulary terms, and the functional language charts, and they can check their own answers with the Answer Key at the back of the *Activity and Resource Book*.

Classroom follow-up will help students consolidate their learning and allow for additional personal attention. As time permits, teachers can also guide the students with the selection of one or more Application Activities which wrap up each unit. Teachers or course coordinators should be sure to monitor students' Progress Checks, to confirm that students are completing each section of the CD-ROM course and are showing ample progress on the review quizzes at the end of each unit.

For additional classroom communication activities, the *Longman English Interactive Communication Companion* is available as both 12 downloadable documents (PDFs) in the CD-ROM course or as a full 48-page, four-color book. The *Longman English Interactive 4 Teacher's Guide*, available for download on the Longman website (www.longman.com/multimedia), provides further suggestions for classroom activities as well as the Web Research and writing assignments for each unit.

The following chart gives an overview of how the sections of the *Longman English Interactive Activity and Resource Book* correspond to the CD-ROM course.

CD-ROM course section	*Activity and Resource Book* corresponding section
Video Listening 1	Listening Exercise A (with Audio CD): a new activity with the same extract
Video Listening 2	Listening Exercise B (with Audio CD): a new activity with the same extract
Vocabulary	Vocabulary: review of vocabulary items in a new context
Speaking	Language Functions: review of the functional language expressions in a new context
Grammar 1	Grammar 1: a review of the grammar point in a new context
Grammar 2	Grammar 2: a review of the grammar point in a new context
Grammar 3	Grammar 3: a review of the grammar point in a new context
Task Listening	Listening Exercise C (with Audio CD): a new activity with the same extract
Pronunciation	
Reading	
Unit Summary Review Quiz	Application Activities

To the Student

Welcome to *Longman English Interactive 4*. This *Activity and Resource Book* will help you with the course.

After you complete each unit of the CD-ROM course, review the unit by doing the exercises in this *Activity and Resource Book*.

Here is a study guide for using the CD-ROM course.

Start at the Course Home.

- Click on the **Orientation** button to download a PDF file with detailed information about using the CD-ROM course.
- Click on the **Course Overview** button to start the course.

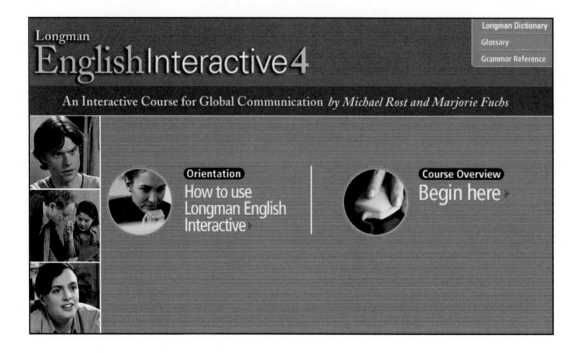

As you go through each unit in the CD-ROM course, try these study tips:

Video Listening

- Watch each video 3 times.
- Use the "pause" button, if necessary.
- Pay attention to the characters' body movements and facial expressions.
- Try the exercises. Check your answers. Click on 🄴 to hear part of the recording again.
- Check the transcript after you finish.

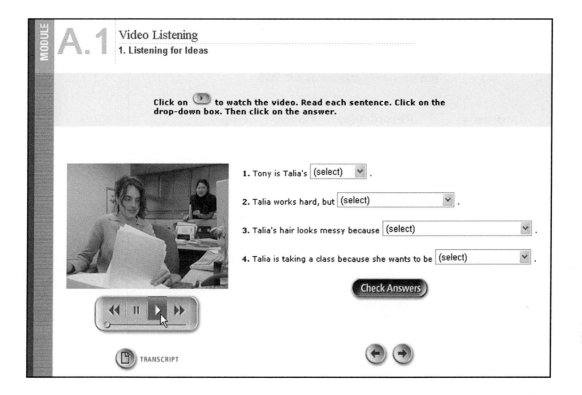

Speaking

- First, listen to the sample conversation on the Role Play Introduction page. Then click to the Role Play page.
- Click on 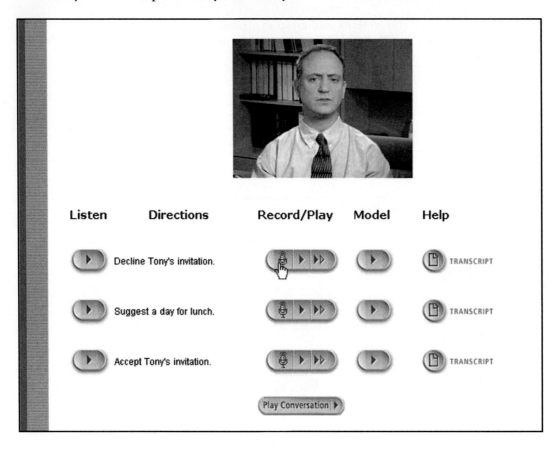 to listen to the character from the video. Read the **directions** for hints on how to respond. Listen to the **model** if you need more help.
- Record your voice. Speak loudly and clearly.

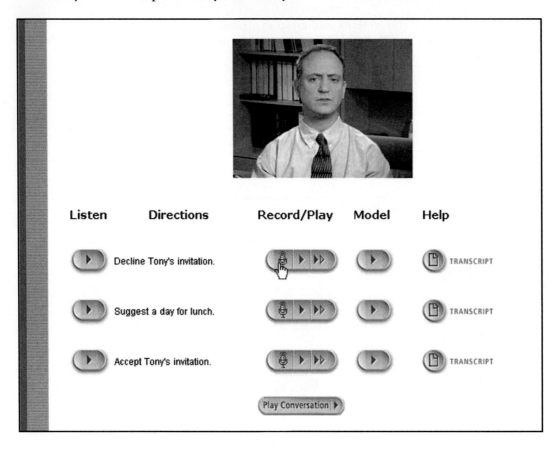

Listen	Directions	Record/Play	Model	Help
▶	Decline Tony's invitation.	🎤 ▶ ▶▶	▶	🗋 TRANSCRIPT
▶	Suggest a day for lunch.	🎤 ▶ ▶▶	▶	🗋 TRANSCRIPT
▶	Accept Tony's invitation.	🎤 ▶ ▶▶	▶	🗋 TRANSCRIPT

Play Conversation ▶

- Play back your voice. Record again if you want.
- Click (Play Conversation ▶) to listen to the entire conversation.
- Try again. This time, use different functional language expressions from the unit.

Grammar

- Listen to the grammar presentations.
- Watch as the words grow, move, and change color. Think about the grammar.
- Use the Grammar Chart and Grammar Help buttons to find out more about the grammar topics.
- Try the exercises. Check your answers. Click on 🄴 for an explanation.

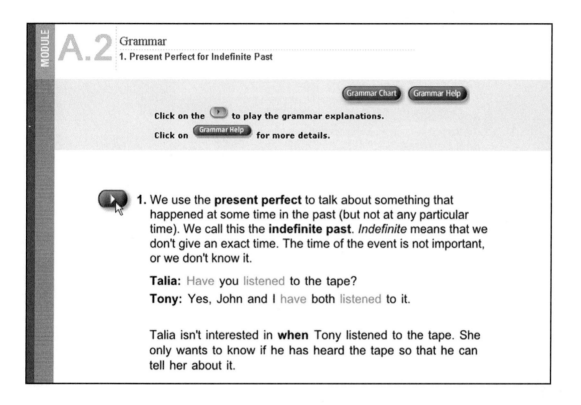

MODULE

A.2 Grammar
1. Present Perfect for Indefinite Past

[Grammar Chart] [Grammar Help]

Click on the ▶ to play the grammar explanations.

Click on [Grammar Help] for more details.

1. We use the **present perfect** to talk about something that happened at some time in the past (but not at any particular time). We call this the **indefinite past**. *Indefinite* means that we don't give an exact time. The time of the event is not important, or we don't know it.

Talia: Have you listened to the tape?
Tony: Yes, John and I have both listened to it.

Talia isn't interested in **when** Tony listened to the tape. She only wants to know if he has heard the tape so that he can tell her about it.

Task Listening

- Click on 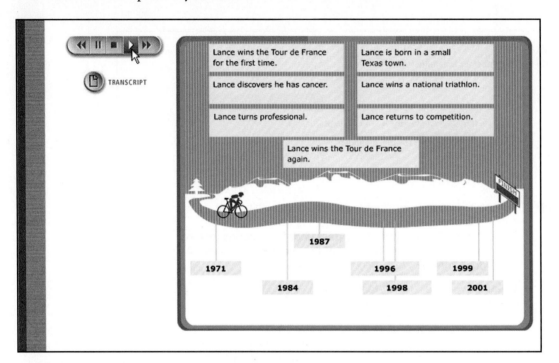 to listen to the recording.
- Use the "pause" button, if necessary.
- Follow the directions to complete the exercise as you listen. You will type in text, click on objects, or drag text from an answer pool on the screen.
- Check the transcript after you finish.

TRANSCRIPT

Lance wins the Tour de France for the first time.

Lance is born in a small Texas town.

Lance discovers he has cancer.

Lance wins a national triathlon.

Lance turns professional.

Lance returns to competition.

Lance wins the Tour de France again.

FINISH

1987

1971

1996

1999

1984

1998

2001

Pronunciation

- Listen to both pronunciation sections and do the practice exercises.
- Record your voice. Compare with the model.

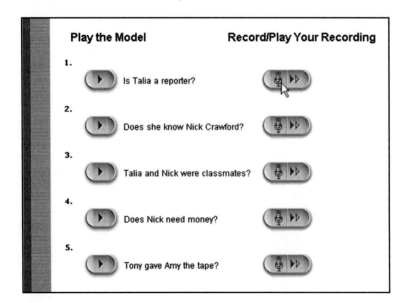

Play the Model   **Record/Play Your Recording**

1. Is Talia a reporter?

2. Does she know Nick Crawford?

3. Talia and Nick were classmates?

4. Does Nick need money?

5. Tony gave Amy the tape?

- Take the review quiz for each unit.
- Check your score. Review the necessary skills if you have any difficulties.

Progress Report

Unit A.1 Review Quiz

Learner's name:

Score: 85%

Language area	Number correct/number of items
Listening for information	6/7
Listening for ideas	2/3
Vocabulary	4/4
Speaking	4/6
Grammar (Simple present vs. present continuous)	4/4

When you use this *Activity and Resource Book*, spend between 50 and 110 minutes on each unit.

Progress Checks

Record your progress for each unit of the CD-ROM course. Make a check (✓) for each activity that you completed. Write your scores for the Review Quiz. (5 minutes)

Listening

Use the Audio CD and do the exercises. (20 minutes)

Vocabulary

Do the Vocabulary exercises. Check the Glossary if necessary. (10 minutes)

Grammar

Review the Grammar Explanations. (10 minutes)

Do the Grammar exercises. (20 minutes)

Language Functions

Review the Language Functions charts.

Do the Language Functions exercises.

Answer Key

Check your answers on pages 129–137. (5 minutes)

Application Activities

Choose two or three activities. Start the activities. (20 minutes— You will need more time for some activities.)

When possible, study with your classmates and your teacher. You can learn a lot of English with *Longman English Interactive*! Have fun using the course.

PROGRESS CHECKS

A.1 The Straight Story

As you complete each section of the CD-ROM course, make a check (✓). Write your scores for the Review Quiz.

Video Listening
_____ **1.** Pre-listening
_____ **1.** Listening for Information
_____ **1.** Listening for Ideas
_____ **2.** Pre-listening
_____ **2.** Listening for Information
_____ **2.** Listening for Ideas

Vocabulary
_____ It's All So Incredible
_____ Practice

Speaking
_____ Language Functions: Directing Conversations
_____ Language Functions: Practice
_____ Role Play 1
_____ Role Play 2

Grammar
_____ **1.** Verb Tense Review
_____ **2.** Negative *Yes/No* Questions and Tag Questions
_____ **3.** Verb (+ Object) + Infinitive

Task Listening
_____ Picture This

Pronunciation
_____ **1.** Unstressed Words (*a, an, the, and, but*)
_____ **2.** The Vowel Sounds in *soon, use,* and *good*

Reading
_____ Pre-reading
_____ Preview vocabulary
_____ Perfect Pitches for International Marketing Success
_____ Comprehension Check

Review Quiz	Score
Listening for information	_____ / 7
Listening for ideas	_____ / 3
Vocabulary	_____ / 4
Speaking	_____ / 6
Grammar 1	_____ / 4
Grammar 2	_____ / 3
Grammar 3	_____ / 3
Pronunciation 1	_____ / 3
Pronunciation 2	_____ / 3
Reading	_____ / 4

A.2 A Hot Lead

As you complete each section of the CD-ROM course, make a check (✓). Write your scores for the Review Quiz.

Video Listening
_____ **1.** Pre-listening
_____ **1.** Listening for Information
_____ **1.** Listening for Ideas
_____ **2.** Pre-listening
_____ **2.** Listening for Information
_____ **2.** Listening for Ideas

Vocabulary
_____ The Bottom Line
_____ Practice

Speaking
_____ Language Functions: Talking about Problems
_____ Language Functions: Practice
_____ Role Play 1
_____ Role Play 2

Grammar
_____ **1.** The Passive
_____ **2.** Quantifiers
_____ **3.** Verb + Gerund or Verb + Infinitive

Task Listening
_____ Job Orientation

Pronunciation
_____ **1.** Falling Intonation for Statements and *Wh-* Questions
_____ **2.** Unstressed Words (*is, was*)

Reading
_____ Pre-reading
_____ Preview vocabulary
_____ IQ vs. EQ: Emotions at work
_____ Comprehension Check

Review Quiz	Score
Listening for information	_____ / 7
Listening for ideas	_____ / 3
Vocabulary	_____ / 4
Speaking	_____ / 6
Grammar 1	_____ / 4
Grammar 2	_____ / 4
Grammar 3	_____ / 2
Pronunciation 1	_____ / 3
Pronunciation 2	_____ / 3
Reading	_____ / 4

Name _____   Date _____

 PROGRESS CHECKS

A.3 Jackie, the Actress

As you complete each section of the CD-ROM course, make a check (✓). Write your scores for the Review Quiz.

Video Listening
_____ **1.** Pre-listening
_____ **1.** Listening for Information
_____ **1.** Listening for Ideas
_____ **2.** Pre-listening
_____ **2.** Listening for Information
_____ **2.** Listening for Ideas

Vocabulary
_____ I Spoke to an Agent
_____ Practice

Speaking
_____ Language Functions: Describing
_____ Language Functions: Practice
_____ Role Play 1
_____ Role Play 2

Grammar
_____ **1.** Present Perfect and Present Perfect Continuous
_____ **2.** Embedded *Wh-* and *Yes/No* Questions
_____ **3.** Participial Adjectives

Task Listening
_____ Registering for Classes

Pronunciation
_____ **1.** Rising Intonation for Some Questions
_____ **2.** Stress in Noun Compounds

Reading
_____ Pre-reading
_____ Preview vocabulary
_____ Cell Phone Phenomenon
_____ Comprehension Check

Review Quiz   **Score**
Listening for information . . . . _____ / 7
Listening for ideas . . . . _____ / 3
Vocabulary . . . . _____ / 4
Speaking . . . . _____ / 6
Grammar 1 . . . . _____ / 4
Grammar 2 . . . . _____ / 3
Grammar 3 . . . . _____ / 3
Pronunciation 1 . . . . _____ / 3
Pronunciation 2 . . . . _____ / 3
Reading . . . . _____ / 4

A.4 A Confrontation

As you complete each section of the CD-ROM course, make a check (✓). Write your scores for the Review Quiz.

Video Listening
_____ **1.** Pre-listening
_____ **1.** Listening for Information
_____ **1.** Listening for Ideas
_____ **2.** Pre-listening
_____ **2.** Listening for Information
_____ **2.** Listening for Ideas

Vocabulary
_____ Piece of Cake
_____ Practice

Speaking
_____ Language Functions: Ending a Conversation
_____ Language Functions: Practice
_____ Role Play 1
_____ Role Play 2

Grammar
_____ **1.** Modals of Possibility and Probability
_____ **2.** Reflexive and Reciprocal Pronouns
_____ **3.** Modals of Possibility and Probability in the Past

Task Listening
_____ Making Reservations

Pronunciation
_____ **1.** Stress in Sentences
_____ **2.** Unstressed Words (*have*)

Reading
_____ Pre-reading
_____ Preview vocabulary
_____ Power Lunch
_____ Comprehension Check

Review Quiz   **Score**
Listening for information . . . . _____ / 7
Listening for ideas . . . . _____ / 3
Vocabulary . . . . _____ / 4
Speaking . . . . _____ / 6
Grammar 1 . . . . _____ / 4
Grammar 2 . . . . _____ / 3
Grammar 3 . . . . _____ / 3
Pronunciation 1 . . . . _____ / 3
Pronunciation 2 . . . . _____ / 3
Reading . . . . _____ / 4

 **PROGRESS CHECKS**

B.1 Talia's Brilliant Plan

As you complete each section of the CD-ROM course, make a check (✓). Write your scores for the Review Quiz.

Video Listening
____ **1.** Pre-listening
____ **1.** Listening for Information
____ **1.** Listening for Ideas
____ **2.** Pre-listening
____ **2.** Listening for Information
____ **2.** Listening for Ideas

Vocabulary
____ In Disguise
____ Practice

Speaking
____ Language Functions: Giving Compliments
____ Language Functions: Practice
____ Role Play 1
____ Role Play 2

Grammar
____ **1.** *Make, Have, Get, Let,* and *Help*
____ **2.** *So* and *Neither*
____ **3.** Future Time Clauses

Task Listening
____ Warning Signals

Pronunciation
____ **1.** Linking Words Together
____ **2.** Stress on Pronouns in Response

Reading
____ Pre-reading
____ Preview vocabulary
____ Spy Gadgetry: Fiction into Fact
____ Comprehension Check

Review Quiz	Score
Listening for information	____ / 7
Listening for ideas	____ / 3
Vocabulary	____ / 4
Speaking	____ / 6
Grammar 1	____ / 4
Grammar 2	____ / 3
Grammar 3	____ / 3
Pronunciation 1	____ / 3
Pronunciation 2	____ / 3
Reading	____ / 4

B.2 Dean's Double Cross

As you complete each section of the CD-ROM course, make a check (✓). Write your scores for the Review Quiz.

Video Listening
____ **1.** Pre-listening
____ **1.** Listening for Information
____ **1.** Listening for Ideas
____ **2.** Pre-listening
____ **2.** Listening for Information
____ **2.** Listening for Ideas

Vocabulary
____ Keep It Down!
____ Practice

Speaking
____ Language Functions: Arguing
____ Language Functions: Practice
____ Role Play 1
____ Role Play 2

Grammar
____ **1.** Simple Past with *When* and Past Continuous with *When*
____ **2.** Reported Imperatives
____ **3.** Subject Adjective Clauses

Task Listening
____ The Way We Met

Pronunciation
____ **1.** Stress on Pronouns for Emphasis or Contrast
____ **2.** Non-final Intonation

Reading
____ Pre-reading
____ Preview vocabulary
____ STRESS!
____ Comprehension Check

Review Quiz	Score
Listening for information	____ / 7
Listening for ideas	____ / 3
Vocabulary	____ / 4
Speaking	____ / 6
Grammar 1	____ / 4
Grammar 2	____ / 3
Grammar 3	____ / 3
Pronunciation 1	____ / 3
Pronunciation 2	____ / 3
Reading	____ / 4

Name _____ Date _____

PROGRESS CHECKS

B.3 Another Confession

As you complete each section of the CD-ROM course, make a check (✓). Write your scores for the Review Quiz.

Video Listening
- ____ **1.** Pre-listening
- ____ **1.** Listening for Information
- ____ **1.** Listening for Ideas
- ____ **2.** Pre-listening
- ____ **2.** Listening for Information
- ____ **2.** Listening for Ideas

Vocabulary
- ____ I Wanted to Ask You Out Then
- ____ Practice

Speaking
- ____ Language Functions: Remembering
- ____ Language Functions: Practice
- ____ Role Play 1
- ____ Role Play 2

Grammar
- ____ **1.** Future Conditional
- ____ **2.** Past Perfect
- ____ **3.** Infinitives after Adjectives and Nouns

Task Listening
- ____ Memories

Pronunciation
- ____ **1.** Stress in Words with *Any-, Every-, Some-, No-*
- ____ **2.** Rising Intonation to Ask for Clarification

Reading
- ____ Pre-reading
- ____ Preview vocabulary
- ____ World Coffee Craze
- ____ Comprehension Check

Review Quiz	**Score**
Listening for information	____ / 7
Listening for ideas	____ / 3
Vocabulary	____ / 4
Speaking	____ / 6
Grammar 1	____ / 4
Grammar 2	____ / 3
Grammar 3	____ / 3
Pronunciation 1	____ / 3
Pronunciation 2	____ / 3
Reading	____ / 4

B.4 A Lesson Learned

As you complete each section of the CD-ROM course, make a check (✓). Write your scores for the Review Quiz.

Video Listening
- ____ **1.** Pre-listening
- ____ **1.** Listening for Information
- ____ **1.** Listening for Ideas
- ____ **2.** Pre-listening
- ____ **2.** Listening for Information
- ____ **2.** Listening for Ideas

Vocabulary
- ____ Get Nick's Name Cleared
- ____ Practice

Speaking
- ____ Language Functions: Troubleshooting
- ____ Language Functions: Practice
- ____ Role Play 1
- ____ Role Play 2

Grammar
- ____ **1.** Future in the Past
- ____ **2.** Passive Causative
- ____ **3.** Reported Statements

Task Listening
- ____ In the News

Pronunciation
- ____ **1.** Stress in Words with Prefixes
- ____ **2.** The Voiced *th* Sound in *This*

Reading
- ____ Pre-reading
- ____ Preview vocabulary
- ____ Stories that Educate and Entertain
- ____ Comprehension Check

Review Quiz	**Score**
Listening for information	____ / 7
Listening for ideas	____ / 3
Vocabulary	____ / 4
Speaking	____ / 6
Grammar 1	____ / 4
Grammar 2	____ / 4
Grammar 3	____ / 2
Pronunciation 1	____ / 3
Pronunciation 2	____ / 3
Reading	____ / 4

Name _____   Date _____

 PROGRESS CHECKS

C.1 A Canceled Celebration

As you complete each section of the CD-ROM course, make a check (✓). Write your scores for the Review Quiz.

Video Listening
_____ **1.** Pre-listening
_____ **1.** Listening for Information
_____ **1.** Listening for Ideas
_____ **2.** Pre-listening
_____ **2.** Listening for Information
_____ **2.** Listening for Ideas

Vocabulary
_____ You're Overreacting
_____ Practice

Speaking
_____ Language Functions: Blaming and Comforting
_____ Language Functions: Practice
_____ Role Play 1
_____ Role Play 2

Grammar
_____ **1.** *Wish*
_____ **2.** Past Unreal Conditional
_____ **3.** *Be supposed to*

Task Listening
_____ Optimist or Pessimist?

Pronunciation
_____ **1.** Reduced Phrases (*supposed to, have to, want to*)
_____ **2.** Unstressed Words (*could, would*)

Reading
_____ Pre-reading
_____ Preview vocabulary
_____ Floral Protocol
_____ Comprehension Check

Review Quiz   **Score**
Listening for information . . . . _____ / 7
Listening for ideas . . . . _____ / 3
Vocabulary . . . . _____ / 4
Speaking . . . . _____ / 6
Grammar 1 . . . . _____ / 3
Grammar 2 . . . . _____ / 4
Grammar 3 . . . . _____ / 3
Pronunciation 1 . . . . _____ / 3
Pronunciation 2 . . . . _____ / 3
Reading . . . . _____ / 4

C.2 Jackie's Big Scene

As you complete each section of the CD-ROM course, make a check (✓). Write your scores for the Review Quiz.

Video Listening
_____ **1.** Pre-listening
_____ **1.** Listening for Information
_____ **1.** Listening for Ideas
_____ **2.** Pre-listening
_____ **2.** Listening for Information
_____ **2.** Listening for Ideas

Vocabulary
_____ Jackie Has Decided to Come Forward
_____ Practice

Speaking
_____ Language Functions: Expressing Feelings About an Event
_____ Language Functions: Practice
_____ Role Play 1
_____ Role Play 2

Grammar
_____ **1.** Present Unreal Conditional
_____ **2.** Past Perfect Continuous
_____ **3.** *Should have*

Task Listening
_____ Interview

Pronunciation
_____ **1.** Reduced Phrases (*should have, could have, would have*)
_____ **2.** Linking Words Together

Reading
_____ Pre-reading
_____ Preview vocabulary
_____ Smile! You're on Candid Camera!
_____ Comprehension Check

Review Quiz   **Score**
Listening for information . . . . _____ / 7
Listening for ideas . . . . _____ / 3
Vocabulary . . . . _____ / 4
Speaking . . . . _____ / 6
Grammar 1 . . . . _____ / 4
Grammar 2 . . . . _____ / 3
Grammar 3 . . . . _____ / 3
Pronunciation 1 . . . . _____ / 3
Pronunciation 2 . . . . _____ / 3
Reading . . . . _____ / 4

Name _____ Date _____

 **PROGRESS CHECKS**

C.3 Hard Evidence

As you complete each section of the CD-ROM course, make a check (✓). Write your scores for the Review Quiz.

Video Listening
_____ **1.** Pre-listening
_____ **1.** Listening for Information
_____ **1.** Listening for Ideas
_____ **2.** Pre-listening
_____ **2.** Listening for Information
_____ **2.** Listening for Ideas

Vocabulary
_____ Jackie Gave Us Hard Evidence
_____ Practice

Speaking
_____ Language Functions: Getting Angry
_____ Language Functions: Practice
_____ Role Play 1
_____ Role Play 2

Grammar
_____ **1.** Future Continuous
_____ **2.** Object Adjective Clauses
_____ **3.** Passive Modals

Task Listening
_____ Nightmare

Pronunciation
_____ **1.** Consonant Clusters
_____ **2.** Stress in Words Ending in *-tion* and *-ate*

Reading
_____ Pre-reading
_____ Preview vocabulary
_____ Proverbs Around the World
_____ Comprehension Check

Review Quiz	**Score**
Listening for information	_____ / 7
Listening for ideas	_____ / 3
Vocabulary	_____ / 4
Speaking	_____ / 6
Grammar 1	_____ / 4
Grammar 2	_____ / 3
Grammar 3	_____ / 3
Pronunciation 1	_____ / 3
Pronunciation 2	_____ / 3
Reading	_____ / 4

C.4 Just Being Honest

As you complete each section of the CD-ROM course, make a check (✓). Write your scores for the Review Quiz.

Video Listening
_____ **1.** Pre-listening
_____ **1.** Listening for Information
_____ **1.** Listening for Ideas
_____ **2.** Pre-listening
_____ **2.** Listening for Information
_____ **2.** Listening for Ideas

Vocabulary
_____ That Reporter Who Broke the Story
_____ Practice

Speaking
_____ Language Functions: Talking About Intentions and Plans
_____ Language Functions: Practice
_____ Role Play 1
_____ Role Play 2

Grammar
_____ **1.** Adjective Clauses: Review and Expansion
_____ **2.** Auxiliary Verbs of Emphasis
_____ **3.** Review of Phrasal Verbs

Task Listening
_____ Congratulations!

Pronunciation
_____ **1.** Stress in Phrasal Verbs
_____ **2.** Vowels Followed by *r*

Reading
_____ Pre-reading
_____ Preview vocabulary
_____ Happy Endings
_____ Comprehension Check

Review Quiz	**Score**
Listening for information	_____ / 7
Listening for ideas	_____ / 3
Vocabulary	_____ / 4
Speaking	_____ / 6
Grammar 1	_____ / 4
Grammar 2	_____ / 2
Grammar 3	_____ / 4
Pronunciation 1	_____ / 3
Pronunciation 2	_____ / 3
Reading	_____ / 4

A.1 | The Straight Story

🎧 **A. Listen to Track 1.** *Nick and Talia are talking about how Nick met Jackie Baker. Complete Nick's story.*

Nick: . . . So, she (1)_____meets_____ me in the

lobby, we (2)_____ hands, and

she (3)_____ me to lunch. . . .

And then she (4)_____ me to

(5)_____ a new pair of shoes.

 . . . And she (6)_____ that I'll

have to (7)_____ the shoes when

I (8)_____. And the company

(9)_____ my name in ads.

🎧 **B. Listen to Track 2.** *Jackie is describing the endorsement deal to Nick. Complete Jackie's explanation.*

Jackie: So you (1)_____ our shoes

when you (2)_____. And we

(3)_____ your name in ads.

(4)_____ that and $50,000

(5)_____ yours. . . . We

(6)_____ the details later for

this, but we'll probably (7)_____

you to appear in a commercial.

C. Listen to Track 3. *You will hear 3 pitches for TV commercials. Listen for the phrases listed in the chart. Which commercial does the phrase appear in? Make a check (✓) in the correct column.*

	Commercial 1: Tropica Tours	Commercial 2: Silver Mountain	Commercial 3: Globaltrek.com
cloudless blue	✓		
bright and glorious			
majestic white			
hugging the mountain			
caresses your face			
perfect harmony			
strolling leisurely			
sparkle in the light			
heart delights			
totally content			

Vocabulary

See Appendix 2 to review the vocabulary terms.

A. *Use prefixes to form opposites of the words in the box. Fill in the chart.*

accurate	credible	likely	regular
attractive	dependent	original	sane
believable	legal	practical	suitable

un-	im-	in-	il-	ir-
unbelievable		incredible		

B. Amy's brother, Mark Lee, is a high school student. Mark wrote this article for his high school newspaper. Replace the words and phrases in bold with words from the chart or the vocabulary list in Exercise A. You won't use all the words.

The High School
Connection

Election This Friday

Who is going to win this year's election for Student President of Taft High School? Polls that were taken last week indicate that the race between Natalie and Alice is close. Of course, the numbers in polls are often (1) ~~wrong~~ *inaccurate*.

It's (2) **improbable** that Natalie Amaya will win the election. Although her ideas are (3) **new and different** and innovative, some think her strategies are (4) **not sensible**. Student Kerry Wise says, "Her idea to have class on Saturday and Sunday is (5) **crazy**! I would never vote for her." However, history teacher Mr. Jenkins admires her. "I think she is a person who is strong and (6) **does not care what other people think**. I admire her."

In my view, it's more (7) **probable** that Alice Wong will win the election. Her plan to reduce class size is very (8) **good** and will benefit the students and the teachers. Others like her for other reasons. "I like her poster design. The colors she chose are very (9) **beautiful**," says student Laura Parkinson. Several students have reported, "I am in favor of her plan to allow the school to put soft-drink machines in classrooms, even though it is currently (10) **against state regulations**."

It's hard to predict who will win right now. Stay tuned and find out next week. Good luck to both candidates!

—Mark Lee, Junior, Class 3D

Grammar 1

Verb Tense Review*

Newsline reporter Claire Adams has just finished a report on the smoothie company, Health Blends. Put each verb in parentheses in the correct tense. Sometimes more than 1 answer is possible.

Health Blends Corporation is in trouble. The smoothie

company (1) **(experience)** ___is experiencing___ problems

with its new line of smoothie drinks called "Green Delights."

The problems (2) **(start)** _____ a few months

ago. While Health Blends (3) **(develop)** _____

Veggie Delights, they realized that consumers weren't buying

it. Nobody (4) **(be)** _____ interested in trying

green health drinks. So, they (5) **(decide)** _____

to hire Thomas Sellers from HotButton Advertising. For Sellers,

throughout his career, the key (6) **(always be)** _____ to listen to consumers.

"The key (7) **(be)** _____ to understand people's tastes," he always says.

"Consumers (8) **(want)** _____ a healthy, delicious drink. So remind them that

Green Delights is not only healthy, but it (9) **(taste)** _____ great, too." Sellers

(10) **(come up with)** _____ a better slogan ("Get into the Green"), a cool

cartoon character ("Green Goddess"), and a new and improved print ad. Health Blends (11)

(run) _____ the new ads tomorrow. Will the new campaign improve sales?

We shall see . . .

*To review the grammar points, see the Grammar Explanations at the end of each unit.

Grammar 2

Study Tip
Review the Grammar Explanations before you do the exercises. Write your own example for 3 grammar points.

Negative *Yes/No* Questions and Tag Questions

A. *Nick Crawford is at the supermarket and some fans recognize him. Complete the conversations with a negative yes/no question or tag question and short answer. Be careful about verb tenses.*

1. **Fan 1:** Excuse me. _____Aren't you_____ Nick Crawford?

   Nick: Yes, _____I am_____. I'm Nick Crawford.

   Fan 1: You're the guy with the gambling problem, _____?

   Nick: No, that's not right. I don't have a gambling problem.

2. **Fan 2:** Nick Crawford? Oh, you play on the national volleyball team, _____?

   Nick: No, _____. Actually, I play on the national soccer team.

3. **Fan 3:** I have a question about Dean Bishop. He isn't as good as you, _____?

   Nick: I can't really say. He's a great player.

4. **Fan 4:** You've been having money problems and taking bribes, _____?

   Nick: No, _____. Those rumors are both untrue.

5. **Fan 5:** But Coach Haskins was on *Sports Night* last night. **(not say)** _____ that you're having some problems?

   Nick: I didn't see the program. I don't know what he said.

6. **Fan 6:** **(not date)** _____ a woman with long, brown, curly hair right now?

   Nick: No, _____. I'm not dating anyone right now.

B. *Now imagine you are talking to your favorite celebrity or athlete. Write one negative yes/no question and one tag question.*

   EXAMPLE: **Star:** _____Angelina Jolie_____

   Your question: _____You have a new movie coming out, don't you?_____

1. **Star:** _____

   Your question: _____

2. **Star:** _____

   Your question: _____

Grammar 3

Verb (+ Object) + Infinitive

A. *Jackie had an audition for a part in a movie. She left a message on her friend's voicemail. Her friend passed on the information to other friends. Fill in the blanks with the correct form of the verb in parentheses. Add an appropriate pronoun where necessary.*

1. **Jackie** (*to Brian*): Brian, I'm really excited. I think Grant Fielding likes me. I definitely expect

   (get) _____to get_____ a small part! Don't tell anybody—it's still a secret!

2. **Brian** (*to Leah*): Guess what, Leah? Jackie Bishop is really excited. She was talking to the casting director for a new movie, a guy named Graham Fielding. Now she expects **(get)**

   _____ a big part!

3. **Leah** (*to Katherine*): Did you hear? Jackie talked with the writer of the play, Gary Fields. She

   convinced **(give)** _____ her the main role!

4. **Katherine** (*to Greg*): You won't believe this! Jackie has the lead role now in a major movie. The head of the studio, Gray Feldman, actually invited **(take)** _____ the lead

   role!

5. **Greg** (*to Jackie*): Hey, congratulations! I heard you met with Greg Feldman. And you agreed

   (take) _____ the lead role in his new movie, *Hearsay*. That's fantastic!

   Jackie: Huh?

BONUS
How did the information change in each conversation?

_____

B. *Now write sentences about yourself. Use verb + object + infinitive expressions. Use some of the verbs in the box. Think about people such as your teacher, your boss, your parents, or your boyfriend/girlfriend/spouse.*

allow	convince	need	expect	teach	want

EXAMPLES: My teacher expects me to study hard.

   I expect my teacher to correct my mistakes.

1. _____

2. _____

Language Functions

See Appendix 3 to review the language function charts.

Amy is talking to her brother Mark about the article he wrote. Fill in the missing parts of the conversations. Use the cues in parentheses and the expressions in the box or other functional expressions from the unit.

What's . . .	Oh, I wanted to . . .	To get back to . . .

Amy: Hi. (1) *(catch up on things)* _____ at school?

Mark: Well, the election for school president is this week. I wrote an article about it for the school newspaper.

Amy: Oh, good for you. You know, I think high school elections are really popularity contests. The person who has the most friends usually wins.

Mark: Yeah, that might be true. Anyway, (2) *(linking back)* _____, the article is due tomorrow. Could you help me edit it?

Amy: Sure, I can do that. (3) *(changing the subject)* _____, I've got an extra ticket to the Crawl concert on Saturday. Want to come along?

Application Activities

1. **Grammar.** Find a news article in a newspaper or a magazine. Make a list of columns for verb tenses: simple present, present continuous, present perfect, simple past, past progressive. As you read the article, underline the verbs. Then make a check (✓) in the appropriate column. What percent of the verbs are in each column?

2. **Vocabulary.** Find more words that can be combined with each negative prefix: *il-, im-, in-, ir-,* and *un-.* Then write sentences using the words and their opposites.

3. **Writing.** Advertisements sometimes make promises that they can't keep about products (for example, a face cream that promises it will "erase your age"). Think of a time when you were disappointed by a product you bought. Write a letter of complaint to the company.

4. **Speaking.** Talk to a person you know. Ask the person what's happening in some area of his or her life. Possible topics include work, school, a relationship, or another person you both know. Use expressions to open the conversation and expressions for catching up on things. For example: *So what's going on with Susie? I haven't heard from her in a while. Is she still in school?*

5. **Project.** Pretend you work for an Advertising Agency called Entice. You are going to develop an idea for a commercial for the company. Write "a pitch" (an advertising theme) for 1 of the items below. Include details about what consumers will see and hear in the ads. Present your pitch to the class (the company's executives). The class will vote on the best pitches.

   • A new ESL language program
   • A weight loss pill
   • Pizza Pop, a new soft drink that tastes just like pizza

Grammar Explanations

This section contains the same grammar explanations that are found on the CD-ROM. They are included here for your quick reference. To view the animated presentation, go to the Grammar section of Unit A.1 in the CD-ROM course.

Grammar 1: Verb Tense Review

1. We use the **present continuous** (*be* + verb + *-ing*) to talk about something that's happening **right now** or **these days**.

   Jackie: I**'m working** on an idea for a commercial **right now**.

2. We use the **simple present** to talk about something that happens **every day** or **all the time**.

   Talia **works** at *Newsline*.

   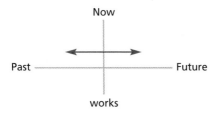

3. We also use the **simple present** with **non-action** verbs like *know*, *believe*, *want*, and *like*—even when we are talking about something that's happening right now.

   Talia: I **want** to hear more about this commercial.

   We do **NOT** say: ~~I'm wanting to hear.~~

4. We can also use the **simple present** when we tell a **story**—even if the story is about the past. The simple present makes the story more dramatic.

   Nick: She **meets** me in the lobby, we **shake** hands, and she **takes** me out to lunch.

5. We usually use the **simple past** to talk about something that happened in the past and is **finished**.

   Nick: I **told** you about that **before**.

6. We often use the simple past with **time expressions** that refer to a **specific time in the past** (for example: *last year, in 1999, 10 years ago*).

   Nick **met** Jackie **several months ago**.

7. We use the **present perfect** (*have* + the past participle) to talk about something that happened at some time in the past (but not at a specific time).

Talia: One of Nick's teammates **has framed** him.

We also use the **present perfect** with *for* or *since* to talk about something that **started in the past and continues to the present**.

We use the present perfect with *for* and a **length of time** to show how long the situation has been going on.

Nick **has been** here **for 2 hours**.

We use the present perfect with *since* and a **point of time** to show when the situation started.

Nick **has been** here since **7:00**.

8. We often use the present perfect with words like *already*, *yet*, *just*, *recently*, and *lately*.

   Nick: I**'ve already told** you.

9. We can also use the **present perfect continuous** (*have* + *been* + verb + *-ing*) to talk about something that **started in the past and continues to the present**.

   Talia: I**'ve been thinking** about this **all day**.

   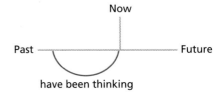

10. As with the present perfect, we often use the present perfect continuous with *for* and *since*.

    Talia **has been working** on this story **for** a few days.

    She**'s been working** on it **since last Monday**.

    Remember, we usually don't use continuous forms with non-action verbs.

    We do **NOT** say: ~~Talia has been having a headache all day.~~

11. We can use *be going to* or *will* to talk about the **future**.

    Talia: I**'ll call** you **tomorrow**.

    Talia **is going to** call her mother **tomorrow**.

Grammar 2: Negative *Yes/No* Questions and Tag Questions

1. We use **negative *yes/no* questions** to check information. We expect the answer to be *yes*.
   Jackie: Aren't you Nick Crawford, the soccer star?
   Nick: Yes.

2. To form a negative *yes/no* question, we add ***not*** to the verb *be* or the auxiliary verb (a form of *do* or *have* or a modal such as *can* or *should*). We almost always use the contraction (short form).
   Aren't you Nick Crawford?

3. We also use **tag questions** to check information.
   Nick: I told you about the commercial, **didn't I?**

4. A tag question is made of a statement and a tag.
   Talia: You went to a restaurant, didn't you?

   You went to a restaurant is the statement. And *didn't you?* is the tag.

5. Notice that the subject of the tag is the same as the subject of the statement.
   Nick: You were in my class, weren't **you?**

   We only use pronouns in the tag.
   Nick: Kicks are cool, aren't **they?**

   We do **NOT** say: ~~Kicks are cool, aren't Kicks?~~

6. When the statement is affirmative, the tag is negative.
   You **were** in my class, **weren't** you?

   You were in my class is affirmative. The tag, *weren't you?*, is negative.

   I'm right, **aren't I?**

7. When the statement is negative, the tag is affirmative.
   You **weren't** in my class, **were** you?

   You weren't in my class is negative. The tag, *were you?*, is affirmative.

8. The tag always has a form of the verb *be* or an auxiliary (a form of *do* or *have* or a modal such as *can* or *should*). If the statement has the verb *be* or an auxiliary verb, we use the same verb in the tag.
   You're a big soccer fan, **aren't** you?
   You **don't** trust me, **do** you?
   We **can** meet again, **can't** we?

   If the statement does not have a form of the verb *be* or an auxiliary verb, we must use a form of *do* in the tag.
   I **know** you, **don't** I?

   Remember that the form of *do* in the tag must be in the same tense as the verb in the statement.
   We **studied** together for the final, **didn't** we?

9. We **answer** negative *yes/no* questions and tag questions the same way we answer affirmative *yes/no* questions. If the information is correct, we say *yes*. If the information is wrong, we say *no*.
   Sam: Aren't you a reporter?
   John: Yes, I am. I'm a reporter for *Newsline*.
   Talia: No, I'm not. I'm a researcher.

Sam: You're a reporter, aren't you?
John: Yes, I am. I'm a reporter for *Newsline*.
Talia: No, I'm not. I'm a researcher.

Tag Questions

Statement	Tag
affirmative	negative
negative	affirmative
noun or pronoun subject	subject always a pronoun
a form of *be*	a form of *be*
an auxiliary verb	the same auxiliary verb
a modal	the same modal
don't or *doesn't*	*do* or *does*
a verb without auxiliary	a form of *do*
same tense as in tag	same tense as in statement

Grammar 3: Verb (+ Object) + Infinitive

1. Some verbs are followed directly by an **infinitive** (*to* plus the base form).
   Nick **agreed to do** a commercial.

Some Verbs Followed Directly by an Infinitive

agree	decide	forget
hope	learn	promise

2. Some verbs must be followed by an **object** (a noun or pronoun) before the **infinitive**.
   Nick: She **convinced me to make** a commercial.

Some Verbs Followed by an Object and an Infinitive

allow	convince	invite
remind	teach	tell

3. Some verbs can be followed directly by an infinitive or by an object and an infinitive.
   Nick: I **want to appear** in a commercial.
   Jackie: I **want you to appear** in a commercial.

Verbs That Can Be Followed by the Infinitive with or without an Object

ask	expect	need
pay	want	would like

A.2 | A Hot Lead

🎧 **A. Listen to Tracks 4 and 5.** *There are several verb + verb combinations in the conversations. Check (✓) the ones you hear.*

Track 4: Talia and Tony at the *Newsline* office

1. __✓__ I need to see you.   ____ I need to talk to you.

2. ____ I forgot to tell you.   ____ I didn't remember to tell you.

3. ____ He resents following Nick.   ____ He resents being in Nick's shadow.

4. ____ He wants to have only one star on the team.   ____ He wants to be the only star on the team.

5. ____ I know you'd like to clear Nick's name.   ____ I know you want to clear Nick's name.

6. ____ If you're planning to have a career . . .   ____ If you want to have a career . . .

7. ____ You have to consider staying objective.   ____ You have to remember to stay objective.

Track 5: Amy and Patty at the juice bar

8. ____ I'm trying to get hold of someone . . .   ____ I'm hoping to get hold of someone . . .

9. ____ She quit coming here a while ago.   ____ She stopped coming here a while ago.

10. ____ I remember talking with him . . .   ____ I remember seeing him . . .

11. ____ I'd rather not talk to him.   ____ I'd rather avoid seeing him.

B. Listen to Track 6. *After listening, complete the sentences. Use the words and phrases in the box. You will not use all the phrases, but you will use some phrases more than once.*

giving options	bad	good
asking	confirming	sympathizing
finding out	using	taking (something) personally

1. Saying "Oh, you must feel terrible" is a good example of _____ with the customer.

2. Asking "When did this happen?" is a good example of _____ exactly what the complaint is.

3. Saying "Thank you, Mr. Smith, for calling today" is a clear example of _____ the customer's name.

4. Saying "I don't believe you!" is a *bad* example of _____ with the customer.

5. Saying "Don't blame me for your problem" is an example of _____ the customer's complaint _____.

6. Asking "What can I do to make this right for you?" is a good example of _____ the customer _____.

7. Saying "Here's what you should do" is a *bad* example of _____ the customer _____.

8. "There's nothing you can do about it" is a _____ example of explaining the customer's options.

9. Saying "So you're saying that . . . ?" is a _____ example of confirming what the customer says.

Vocabulary

See Appendix 2 to review the vocabulary terms.

During her free time at the juice bar, Patty writes emails to her friends. Replace the phrases in bold with phrases from the word box. Be sure to use the correct verb tense.

along the same lines	be out of line	down the line	drop you a line
get a line on	give me a line	lay it on the line	take a hard line

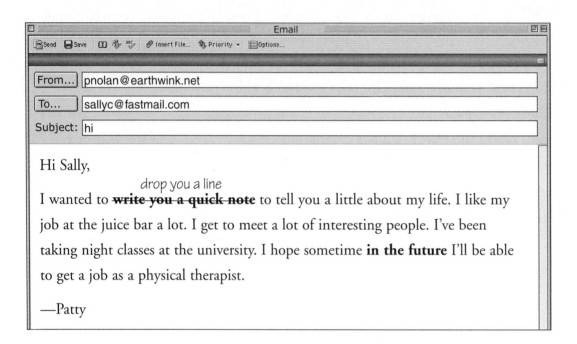

Email

Send Save   Insert File... Priority ▾   Options...

From... pnolan@earthwink.net

To... sallyc@fastmail.com

Subject: hi

Hi Sally,

drop you a line
I wanted to **write you a quick note** to tell you a little about my life. I like my job at the juice bar a lot. I get to meet a lot of interesting people. I've been taking night classes at the university. I hope sometime **in the future** I'll be able to get a job as a physical therapist.

—Patty

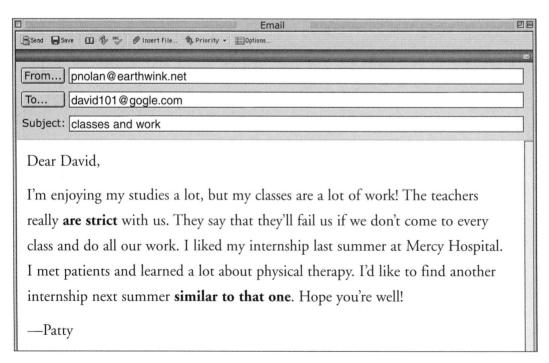

Email

Send Save   Insert File... Priority ▾   Options...

From... pnolan@earthwink.net

To... david101@gogle.com

Subject: classes and work

Dear David,

I'm enjoying my studies a lot, but my classes are a lot of work! The teachers really **are strict** with us. They say that they'll fail us if we don't come to every class and do all our work. I liked my internship last summer at Mercy Hospital. I met patients and learned a lot about physical therapy. I'd like to find another internship next summer **similar to that one**. Hope you're well!

—Patty

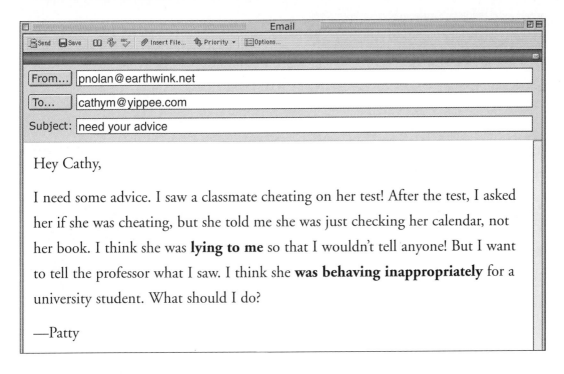

Email

From... | pnolan@earthwink.net
To... | cathym@yippee.com
Subject: | need your advice

Hey Cathy,

I need some advice. I saw a classmate cheating on her test! After the test, I asked her if she was cheating, but she told me she was just checking her calendar, not her book. I think she was **lying to me** so that I wouldn't tell anyone! But I want to tell the professor what I saw. I think she **was behaving inappropriately** for a university student. What should I do?

—Patty

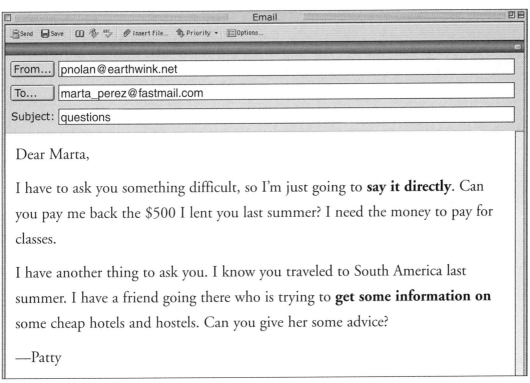

Email

From... | pnolan@earthwink.net
To... | marta_perez@fastmail.com
Subject: | questions

Dear Marta,

I have to ask you something difficult, so I'm just going to **say it directly**. Can you pay me back the $500 I lent you last summer? I need the money to pay for classes.

I have another thing to ask you. I know you traveled to South America last summer. I have a friend going there who is trying to **get some information on** some cheap hotels and hostels. Can you give her some advice?

—Patty

The Passive

Claire is doing some research for a travel article about Italy. Each sentence contains 1 error. Correct the error.

1. The Leaning Tower of Pisa was designed ^by Bonanno Pisano.

2. In 1999, the Tower visited by a million people.

3. Because of wars in Italy, workers were stopped construction on the Tower several times.

4. In 1995, 600 tons of lead is added to the Tower.

5. In 1178, people were noticed that the Tower was tilted.

6. In 1273, the architect Pontedera was realized that the tower couldn't be straightened.

7. In 1990, the Italian government was closed the Tower to the public.

8. In 2001, the Leaning Tower of Pisa reopened by the government.

BONUS
Write 2 or 3 sentences about a famous place in your city or country. Make some sentences active and some passive. Use the sentences in Exercise A as an example.

_____

_____

Grammar 2

Quantifiers

A. *Fill in the blanks in each pair of sentences. Choose 1 of the words in parentheses and change it to the correct form when necessary.*

1. **(word, vocabulary)** Luisa knows a lot of _____ in English. Her _____ is huge.

2. **(problem, help)** Can you give me some _____? I can't answer some of these _____.

3. **(drink, tea)** Can I have a _____ please? I'd like some _____.

4. **(question, information)** I need some _____. Could you answer some _____ for me, please?

5. **(dollar, money)** This watch is worth a lot of _____. I'll give you a hundred _____ for it.

B. *Is each noun <u>usually</u> countable or non-countable? Write* **C** *(count) or* **NC** *(non-count).*

_____ advice	_____ information	_____ music
_____ baggage	_____ knowledge	_____ song
_____ education	_____ love	_____ time
_____ experience	_____ loyalty	_____ vocabulary
_____ idea	_____ minute	_____ work

Grammar 3

Verb + Gerund or Verb + Infinitive

Jackie and Dean remember some things about their childhood, but they don't remember other things. Fill in each blank with the correct form of the verb in parentheses—a gerund or an infinitive. If both are possible, write both.

1. When Jackie was little, she loved **(wait)** ___to wait/waiting___ by the window for the ice cream truck to come around on hot summer days.

2. She was so excited when she heard the truck coming, she often forgot **(put on)** _____ her shoes. She ran out into the street without them.

3. Jackie really enjoyed **(play)** _____ with her dolls.

4. She liked **(pretend)** _____ that she was an actress and her dolls were her audience.

5. Sometimes she continued **(talk)** _____ to them for hours. She wouldn't stop **(talk)** _____ until her mother called her for dinner.

6. When Jackie was 7 years old, she started **(perform)** _____ plays for her family in the living room.

7. She wanted **(be)** _____ the star of the family, but little Dean didn't like **(share)** _____ the attention with his sister.

8. As a child, Dean was an excellent athlete. He wanted his parents **(watch)** _____ his soccer matches, but they seldom managed **(attend)** _____.

9. Both Dean and Jackie remember **(compete)** _____ for their parents' attention.

BONUS

Think about your childhood. Write about what people have told you that you did when you were a small child. Write 2 things you remember and two things you forget having done.

_____   _____

_____   _____

Language Functions

See Appendix 3 to review the language function charts.

Replace each phrase in bold with a similar phrase. There is always more than 1 acceptable answer.

Study Tip
Choose 3 Application Activities. Complete the activities this week!

Patty: (1) ~~You look depressed.~~ *You seem upset.* (2) **Are you OK?**

Andrea: Well, it's my history class. (3) **I'm nervous about** the final exam.

Patty: (4) **I have an idea**. (5) **Why don't you** form a study group with some of your classmates?

Andrea: (6) **Hmm . . . that might work**.

Patty: Miguel, (7) **you seem like you've got a problem**. Is everything all right?

Miguel: (8) **I'm stressed out about** my wedding. I think Kimiko and I are going to spend too much money on it.

Patty: (9) **If I were you, I'd** talk to Kimiko. Maybe you can invite just a few guests.

Miguel: (10) **No, that won't work**. She's already invited over 100 people!

Application Activities

1. **Grammar and Vocabulary.** Keep a grammar notebook. Make a heading for this category: *Non-count nouns*. How many non-count nouns do you know? Look at a newspaper or magazine article or at a news website. Add all the non-count nouns you can find. Try to add to your list each week.

2. **Grammar.** In your grammar notebook, make a list with 3 categories: *Verbs that are followed by a gerund, Verbs that are followed by an infinitive,* and *Verbs that are followed by either a gerund or an infinitive.* Write several verbs in each category. Then say at least 10 sentences using verb combinations. Record the sentences on tape. Play the sentences back and check your own grammar.

3. **Writing.** It's important in many jobs to stay objective—not to get emotional. Explain how objectivity may be important in 1 of the following jobs: teacher, historical researcher, chemist/biologist, marriage counselor/psychiatrist, doctor, police officer.

4. **Speaking.** Talk to 2 people about a problem you are having. Use expressions for talking about the situation and feelings. Listen for expressions the person uses to express a solution. Compare the 2 pieces of advice you get.

5. **Project.** Find out about a famous person from business, entertainment, education, or politics. Use books, magazines, or websites to look for information. Write down at least 5 key facts or ideas about the person. Give a short presentation to your class.

Grammar Explanations

This section contains the same grammar explanations that are found on the CD-ROM. They are included here for your quick reference. To view the animated presentation, go to the Grammar section of Unit A.2 in the CD-ROM course.

Grammar 1: The Passive

1. We form the **passive** with a form of *be* + **the past participle** of the verb.
   Nick **was tricked**.
   The juice bar **is managed** by Patty.
   The iced tea **is made** fresh every day.

2. An **active** sentence focuses on the agent (the "doer") of an action. A **passive** sentence focuses on the "receiver" of an action. Look at this active sentence:
   Someone tricked **Nick**.

   In the example, *someone* is the agent, and *Nick* is the receiver of the action (the object).

   If we want to focus on Nick, we use a passive sentence.
   Nick **was tricked**.

   Notice that the object of the active sentence (*Nick*) becomes the subject of the passive sentence. Notice, too, that the subject (*Nick*) must agree with the verb (*was*).

3. We often use the passive when we don't know who the agent is.
   Talia: The tape **was edited**.

   In the example, Talia doesn't know who edited the tape.

4. We can also use the passive when it's clear who the agent is so we don't need to say it.
   The news **is reported** on several channels.

   In the example, we know that reporters report the news, so we do not need to mention the agent.

   We do **NOT** say: ~~The news is reported on several channels by reporters.~~

5. We can also use the passive when we don't want to say who the agent is.
   Tony: Too many mistakes **were made** in that report.

   In the example, Tony doesn't want to say who made the mistakes.

6. Sometimes the name of the agent is important information that we need in the sentence. If we want to say the name of the agent, we use *by*.
   Talia: Nick was tricked **by Jackie Baker**.
   Amy: The story was reported **by John Donnelly**.

Grammar 2: Quantifiers

1. **Count nouns** are nouns that we can count. Here are some examples:
1 friend	10 **friends**
1 member	50 **members**
1 idea	2 **ideas**

   We can use *a lot of*, *many*, and *a few* with plural count nouns.
   Talia: Nick has **a lot of friends** on the team.
   Nick: Do you know **many members** of the team, Patty?
   Talia: I have **a few ideas**.

2. **Non-count nouns** are nouns that we cannot count. Here are some examples:
   help
   information
   money
   tea
   time

   We use *a lot of*, *much*, and *a little* with non-count nouns.
   Tony: It's worth **a lot of money**.
   Tony: We don't have **much time**.
   Talia: I need **a little help** from Amy.

3. Notice that we can use *a lot of* with both count and non-count nouns.
   Talia: Nick has **a lot of friends**.
   Tony: He has **a lot of money**, too.

   We can use *a lot of* in questions and in affirmative or negative statements.
   Talia: **Does** Dean **have a lot of** friends?
   Amy: I **don't have a lot of** money.

4. We usually use *many* and *much* in questions and negative statements rather than in affirmative statements.
   John: I haven't bought my ticket for the game yet. How **much** time do I have**?**
   Tony: They did**n't** have **many** tickets left yesterday. You'd better buy one now.

Grammar 3: Verb + Gerund or Verb + Infinitive

1. You've already learned about **gerunds** and **infinitives**. After some verbs, you have to use the **gerund** (**verb + *-ing***).
   Talia: Dean **resents being** in Nick's shadow.

2. After other verbs, you have to use the **infinitive** (***to* + verb**).
   Talia: He **wants to be** the only star on the team.

3. But some verbs can be followed by either **the gerund or the infinitive**.
   Amy **loves helping** Talia with the story.
   OR
   Amy **loves to help** Talia with the story.

   These 2 sentences have the same meaning.

4. A few verbs can be followed by **the gerund or the infinitive**, but **the meanings are not the same**. Some of these verbs are *forget*, *remember*, and *stop*.

> **Talia:** I **forgot to tell** you.

In this example, Talia didn't tell Tony something. She planned to tell him, but she didn't do it.

> **Talia:** I **forgot telling** you.

In this example, Talia told Tony something, but she didn't remember that she did it.

> **Riv:** Amy **remembered to see** Patty at the health club. Patty told her something interesting.

First Amy remembered to go see Patty. Then she did it.

> **Evan:** Patty **remembered seeing** Dean yesterday.

First Patty saw Dean. Then she remembered that she saw him.

> **Chloe:** Patty **stopped to talk** to Amy.

Patty stopped working so that she could talk to Amy.

> **Zac:** Jackie **stopped coming** to the health club a while ago.

This means that Jackie doesn't come to the health club anymore.

A.3 Jackie, the Actress

Listening

🎧 **A. Listen to Track 7.** *Amy is at the university waiting for Talia. She begins a conversation with Jackie. Fill in the blanks in the conversation.*

Talia: Well, just go over to her and start a conversation.

(1)_____You've done_____ your homework, haven't you?

Amy: My homework?

Talia: I mean, (2)_____ what courses she's taking, and everything?

* * *

Jackie: (3)_____ classes here for about a year and I think he's been my best teacher.

Amy: I know what you mean. He's very . . . inspiring.

Jackie: Yes, absolutely. (4)_____ a much better actor since I started taking his classes . . .

Amy: Yes, I'm sure you (5)_____.

🎧 **B. Listen to Track 8.** *Amy and Jackie continue to talk. Fill in the blanks in the conversation.*

Amy: Oh, I'm Amy Lee, (1)_____.

Jackie: Hi. I'm Jackie Bishop. Well, that's my (2)_____. My (3)_____ is Jackie Baker.

Amy: So do you have an (4)_____?

Jackie: As a matter of fact, I spoke to an agent last week. I just (5)_____ him a (6)_____, and he thought it was (7)_____.

Amy: I'm (8)_____. You do seem . . . incredible.

🎧 **C. Listen to Track 9.** *You will hear an explanation of how to register for classes. Check (✓) the verbs you hear.*

____ register	____ verify	____ means	____ look up	____ enter	____ wait
____ go	____ bring	____ take	____ need	____ select	
____ show	____ give	____ ask	____ log on	____ hurry	

Vocabulary

See Appendix 2 to review the vocabulary terms.

A. Put the words in the box into the following lists according to their form or spelling. Words may be used more than once. (Compound words are made up of 2 words joined together.)

agent	film director	producer	set designer
cameraperson	makeup artist	scriptwriter	stuntperson
costume designer			

Compound word	Two separate words	Ends in *-er*	Ends in *-or*
cameraperson	_____	_____	_____
_____	_____	_____	_____
_____	_____	_____	_____
_____	_____	_____	_____
_____	_____	_____	_____

B. On the Set *is a magazine for people who work in film and theater. In the back of the magazine, there are job advertisements. Read the advertisements, and write the name of the job they describe.*

ON THE SET
AN ACTOR'S RESOURCE

1. scriptwriter — Looking for someone to change a popular novel into an exciting script. Must be creative.

2. ____ — Rosewood Players will present *Into the Woods* this summer. Looking for someone to build the scenery.

3. ____ — Looking for someone to perform a dangerous motorcycle act for new action movie. Must be in great condition and have experience in sport safety.

4. ____ — I am an actress looking for someone to manage my career. Must be organized and have a lot of contacts in the movie industry.

5. ____ — Looking for an extra person to operate modern digital camera on location. Must have experience.

6. ____ — Looking for someone who knows a lot about fashion of the early 1900s and all European styles.

7. ____ — I'm finally making my novel into a movie. I wrote the script, and I'm looking for someone to direct it.

8. ____ — Challenging work for *Monster Ball!* Cast of 100 needs to be made up to look like monsters.

9. ____ — We are making a film about our travels through Asia. We have a scriptwriter, a director, and all of our actors. We are looking for a sponsor.

Grammar 1

Present Perfect and Present Perfect Continuous

A. *Talia, Amy, and Josh are celebrity-watching at Valentino's restaurant. Fill in the blanks with the present perfect or present perfect progressive of the verbs in parentheses.*

Josh: (1) **(notice)** _____ Has _____ anyone _____ noticed _____ Evangelina Belle over there at the corner table? She **(talk)** _____ 's been talking _____ to that mysterious man for over an hour. Do you think they're a couple?

Amy: I (2) **(watch)** _____ her, too. I don't know if they're a couple, but they certainly **(discuss)** _____ something very serious.

Talia: Do you realize that she (3) **(not touch)** _____ her plate of pasta?

Amy: Evangelina may not be hungry, but Myra Banks sure is. She (4) **(eat)** _____ an entire steak, 2 bowls of salad, and a basket of bread.

Josh: And she (5) **(work on)** _____ that piece of double fudge cake for only a few minutes; it's almost half gone!

Amy: Look! There's that Australian playboy, Russel Byrd! He (6) **(live)** _____ in the United States since 2001.

Amy: Russel (7) **(date)** _____ at least 7 different famous women. The last one was Evangelina Belle. You know, Talia, I think he likes you. He (8) **(smile)** _____ at you for the past couple of minutes.

Talia: Get outta here! He (9) **(be)** _____ happily married for 2 years now.

Josh: (10) **(listen)** _____ anyone _____ to the argument between that waiter and that customer over there?

Amy: Yes. How could we miss it?! They (11) **(shout)** _____ at each other for 10 minutes. Wait . . . oh, my gosh! That's Bryce Sprillis yelling at the waiter!

Talia: Oh, look! The manager's coming out. He's talking to the waiter and the waiter looks really upset. I think he (12) **(be)** _____ fired!

B. *Write 3 sentences about yourself using the present perfect and present perfect progressive.*

EXAMPLE: ___ I've been studying English for about 8 years. _____

1. _____

2. _____

3. _____

Grammar 2

Embedded *Wh-* and *Yes/No* Questions

In Jackie's class today, Professor Roberts is explaining how to improvise (how to act without a script). Correct the mistakes in the questions.

1. Do you know why ~~is learning improvisation techniques important.~~ learning improvisation techniques is important?

2. Sometimes a casting director wants to know do you understand the character?

3. The director may ask you to improvise to see are you able to develop a natural feeling for the character?

4. You might ask how can you know what to say?

5. First, you must really get to know your character. When you have discovered who is really the character, you will know how does the character behave. Then improvisation will be easy.

6. I wonder would anyone in the class like to try it?

Grammar 3

Participial Adjectives

A. *Below and on the next page are the reviews for 3 movies and the reactions of people who saw them. Complete the ending of each verb with -ed or -ing to make participial adjectives.*

> *The Green Eye of Jealousy* is a story about a woman, Jean Knight, whose jealousy ruins her life and the lives of others around her. You will be moved by this Oscar-winning movie, which reveals the shocking truth about the power of human emotions to inspire good or evil.

1. **Dean Bishop:** What a bor_ing_ story! I almost fell asleep. This stuff never happens in real life!

2. **Roshawn:** I found the main character very irritat_____. I couldn't stand the way she talked.

3. **Coach Haskins:** I would have been more interest_____ if a better actress had played the part of Jean's sister.

Hearts on the Line is a fantastic romantic comedy about 3 lonely women who agree to team up in their search for love. Inspired by the romantic tales of an old gypsy neighbor, the women agree to play "matchmaker" for each other. However, their choices for each other turn out to be better choices for themselves.

4. **Claire:** The ending was really satisf____. All the main characters find true love.

5. **Ms. Boyd:** The man who plays Judith's true love is amaz____! He is so good-looking and charming. He reminds me of John Donnelly . . .

6. **Amy:** I'm a little embarrass____. I don't want the people at work to know I saw this!

Dead End is about a group of vampires who take over a town in North Carolina. Our hero must spend a horrifying night battling the evil vampires for control of the town. Beware: The action scenes are probably the most terrifying yet in a vampire movie!

7. **Talia:** I was really disappoint____. I thought there would be a lot more action.

8. **Ms. Boyd:** Of course, I wasn't frighten____. I had to leave the theater in the middle of the battle scenes because I needed some more popcorn. And I wasn't screaming because I was afraid—I was just excit____.

Study Tip
Use the CD-ROM Progress Checks on pages xvii–xxii. Look at your Review Quiz scores to see where you need more practice.

B. *Describe 2 of your favorite movies or books. Use participial adjectives and some of the verbs in the box.*

touch	move	inspire	satisfy	amaze	interest
relax	horrify	frighten	entertain	amuse	bore

EXAMPLE: Forrest Gump was a moving film. I was touched by Forrest's simple but amazing life.

1. _____

2. _____

Language Functions

See Appendix 3 to review the language function charts.

Replace the phrases in bold in each conversation with an expression from the language function charts. Use the cues in parentheses.

Marie: **What do you think of** the play you're acting in now?

1. (impression) _____What's your impression of_____

Jackie: It's great. I really like it. I think the director is wonderful.

Marie: **What do you like about** that director?

2. (special) _____

Jackie: Well, he really knows how to draw emotion from the actors.

Marie: **What is your opinion of** the changes to the script?

3. (take) _____

Jackie: I think the changes make the whole play better.

Elisa: Did you like the movie we saw last night?

Tony: Some parts I did, and some parts I didn't.

Elisa: And the music? How did you like it?

Tony: The music was **so-so**, in my opinion.

4. (right) _____

Application Activities

1. **Grammar.** Pick a famous movie or book you have never seen or read. Write statements and questions about it using embedded questions: For example, *Can you tell me how the heroes win the battle at the end of* Lord of the Rings? *I wonder if the third* Lord of the Rings *movie is better than the second.*

2. **Vocabulary.** Build a "word web" for a profession. Start with the entertainment industry: filmmaking. Use the vocabulary list from the unit: *agent, cameraperson, film director,* and so on. How many new job titles can you think of? Find out new jobs by looking at magazines or film websites.

3. **Writing.** Write a movie review of a movie you have seen recently. Take notes after you see the movie. Talk to other people who have also seen the movie. Be sure to include your ideas about the story, the actors, and the music.

4. **Speaking.** Ask several people their impressions of current events or people in the news (for example, an actor, a politician, or a big event) or anything in your personal life (a teacher, a piece of clothing you're wearing, and so on). Use expressions for asking about impressions and responding to questions about impressions.

5. **Project.** The CD-ROM reading in this unit is about new communications technologies. What kinds of communication technologies do you think have a bad effect on society? Do you think the government should regulate technology? For example, should cell phone use in public places be banned by the government? Prepare an argument and present it to the class.

Grammar Explanations

This section contains the same grammar explanations that are found on the CD-ROM. They are included here for your quick reference. To view the animated presentation, go to the Grammar section of Unit A.3 in the CD-ROM course.

Grammar 1: Present Perfect and Present Perfect Continuous

1. We often use the **present perfect** to talk about something that was completed at some time in the past (but not at a specific time). With the present perfect, we are focusing on the **completion and result** of an action.

    Talia: **Have** you **found out** Jackie's schedule?

    In the example, Talia wants to know about the result of Amy's search.

2. We often use the **present perfect continuous** to talk about something that happened in the past and is **still happening**. With the present perfect continuous, we are focusing on the **continuation** of an action.

    Amy: She**'s been sitting** in the lounge for about 10 minutes.

    In the example, Amy means that Jackie is still sitting in the lounge.

3. We often use the **present perfect** to talk about amounts—*how much*, *how many*, and *how many times*.

    Jackie: We**'ve read 3 books** in Professor Roberts's class.

4. We often use the **present perfect continuous** to talk about *how long*.

    Amy: I**'ve been studying** journalism **for about 6 months**.

5. Sometimes you can use either the **present perfect** or the **present perfect continuous**. With verbs such as *live, work, study, play, take*, or *teach* with *for* or *since*, there is often no difference in meaning between the present perfect and the present perfect continuous.

    Amy **has studied** journalism **since** last year.

    Amy **has been studying** journalism **since** last year.

    These 2 sentences have the same meaning.

Grammar 2: Embedded *Wh-* and *Yes/No* Questions

1. An **embedded question** is a question that's **inside another sentence**.

    Amy: What do you mean?
    I know **what** you **mean**.

    What you mean is an embedded question.

2. **Embedded *wh-* questions** begin with a **question word**.

    Amy: When does the class begin?
    Can you tell me **when the class begins**?

3. **Embedded *yes/no* questions** begin with *if*.

    Talia: Is she there?
    Do you know **if she's there**?

4. Notice that we use **statement word order**, not question order, in embedded questions.

    Talia: Where is she?
    Do you know **where she is**?
    Is she there?
    Do you know **if she's there**?

5. We do not use a form of the **auxiliary verb *do*** in the embedded question.

    Amy: What do you mean?
    I know **what** you **mean**.

    We do **NOT** say: ~~I know what do you mean~~ OR ~~I know what you do mean.~~

    Amy: Does she have an agent?
    I wonder **if she has an agent**.

    We do **NOT** say: ~~I wonder does she have an agent.~~ OR ~~I wonder she does have an agent.~~

6. You can have an embedded question inside a statement or inside another question.

    When the **embedded question** is **in a statement**, use a **period** at the end of the sentence.

    I know what you want.

    When the **embedded question** is **in a question**, use a **question mark** at the end of the sentence.

    Can you tell me what you want?

Grammar 3: Participial Adjectives

1. **Participial adjectives** end in *-ed* and *-ing*. They usually describe feelings or reactions, but the two forms have different meanings.

    Examples of participial adjectives are *bored* and *boring*.

Participial Adjectives	
amaz**ed**	amaz**ing**
depress**ed**	depress**ing**
supris**ed**	supris**ing**

2. We use **-ed adjectives** to talk about how someone **feels**.
>   **Amy:** I'm not **surprised**.

   In the example, Amy is talking about how she feels.

3. We use **-ing adjectives** to talk about someone or something that **causes a feeling or reaction**.
>   **Jackie:** I saw Madonna. It was so **exciting**!

   In the example, Jackie is talking about how seeing Madonna in a restaurant caused a reaction in her. Seeing Madonna was *exciting*. As a result, Jackie felt *excited*.

A.4 A Confrontation

Listening

🎧 **A. Listen to Track 10.** *Talia arrives at the university and joins the conversation with Amy and Jackie. Fill in the blanks in the conversation.*

Talia: Gee, you look so familiar.

Jackie: Really? We (1)_____might have seen_____ each other around campus.

Talia: I guess so. Or we (2)_____ in a class together. I'm taking journalism classes.

Jackie: No, it (3)_____ a class. I'm taking acting classes, like Amy.

Talia: Oh, well. I'll probably think of it later.

Jackie: Speaking of classes, (4)_____ run. I don't want to be late for Professor Roberts.

Talia: Hold it. I think I remember where (5)_____ you.

Jackie: Really?

Talia: Yes. The Gower Building.

🎧 **B. Listen to Track 11.** *Talia and Amy continue talking after Jackie leaves. Fill in the blanks in the conversation.*

Talia: So what did you find out?

Amy: Listen to this. Jackie and Dean are going to Valentino's (1)_____ her class tonight to (2)_____. She's booked a special table.

Talia: This is (3)_____. Great work. You should be (4)_____.

Amy: Thanks, but it was nothing. Piece of (5)_____, in fact.

C. Listen to Track 12. *Three callers are making reservations at a restaurant. Number the questions in order for each conversation.*

Caller 1

_____ And your name, please?

_____ How many are in your party?

_____ Which do you prefer?

_____ May I help you?

_____ For when, ma'am?

Caller 2

_____ How many in your party, sir?

_____ Could I have the name of the party, please?

_____ Is that all right?

_____ Can I help you?

_____ For this evening?

Caller 3

_____ For what time, please?

_____ And how many in your party this evening?

_____ And what can I help you with today?

_____ And would you like a table in the main dining room . . . ?

Vocabulary

See Appendix 2 to review the vocabulary terms.

A. *Put each food word in the box into the correct blank.*

apple	bananas	beef	butter	cake
cookie	egg	grapes	pie	potatoes

Make something stronger

Say something nice so someone will do what you want

Something not very important

An attitude of criticizing what you can't have

Very easy

A plan that you think will never happen

Become angry or excited

To be embarrassed from something you said

An intelligent and confident person

Someone who has a bad effect on others

1. _____*beef*_____ something up

2. _____ someone up

3. small _____

4. sour _____

5. a piece of _____

6. _____ in the sky

7. go _____

8. have _____ on your face

9. a smart _____

10. a rotten _____

B. *Patty is writing a letter to her friend to update her about her life. Read the letter. Replace the underlined phrases with food idioms.*

> Dear Kris,
>
> Hey! How's it going with you? I'm doing well. The new semester just started. I'm taking a few easy classes, because I want to (1) <u>make my grade point average stronger</u>. One of my classes is really tough. I met an interesting guy named Kaz in that class (Advanced Biology). He always gets A's—he's really (2) <u>intelligent</u>! So I asked him to be my study partner. We studied a lot together. The first test was very difficult for me, but Kaz thought it was (3) <u>extremely easy</u>. I got a B–, and I was so excited! He got a B+, and he couldn't believe it! He (4) <u>was really angry and upset</u>. I told him not to worry about it, that the exam (5) <u>wasn't that important</u>. There's more to life than school!
>
> Write back soon!
> Love, Patty

1. _____

2. _____

3. _____

4. _____
5. _____

Grammar 1

Modals of Possibility and Probability

Amy and her friends are at Valentino's to watch celebrities. Choose the best verb or the best modal of possibility/probability. For some choices, there is more than 1 correct modal.

1. **Josh:** Is that Brad Pruit, the famous actor?

   Amy: It looks like him, but he's wearing dark sunglasses and a hat. If it *is* Brad Pruit, he **shouldn't be / won't be /(must be)** afraid someone is going to recognize him. Otherwise, why would he wear a disguise?

2. **Claire:** Poor guy! He **can need / can't need / must need** privacy in his life, just like everybody else!

3. **Amy:** You know, I'm not sure who that is. It **can't be / won't be / might not be** Brad Pruit after all. It **is / will be / may be** Anton Bandera. Or it **is / will be / might be** Donny Jepp! It's just too hard to tell.

4. **Josh:** There's Lisbeth Tyler. She **couldn't be / might not be / must be** on a diet. All she ordered was a bowl of soup and she definitely **looks / may look / must look** thinner than the last time I saw her in a movie.

5. **Amy:** Oh, Josh! Don't you know people always look heavier in films?! Besides, she **won't be / can't be / may not be** on a diet.

   Claire: That's right. Lizzie **may not believe / won't believe / doesn't believe** in diets. I heard her say that in a TV interview recently.

6. **Claire:** **Could that be / Would that be / Should that be** Tiger Forrest, the famous golfer?

   Josh: Yes, **that's / that may be / that might be** him. I'm sure it's him.

7. **Amy:** No. It **can't be / might not be / mustn't be**. Tiger just shaved his head, and that guy's got long hair.

8. **Josh:** Look. There goes Brad Pruit, or whoever!

   Claire: He **realized / probably realized / may have realized** that we recognized him. You know, we shouldn't stare at him. This kind of stress **isn't / can't be / must not be** good for him!

Grammar 2

Reflexive and Reciprocal Pronouns

Correct the mistakes in the use of reflexive pronouns (myself, yourselves, *etc.*) *and reciprocal pronouns* (each other, one another). *Note: In some sentences, object pronouns* (him, her, it, *etc.*) *should be used instead.*

1. Amy and Patty hadn't met before, so they introduced ~~each other~~. ^{themselves}
2. Tony and his wife, Elisa, encourage another to eat healthy food.
3. Jackie wanted to celebrate something with Dean. So she bought herself an expensive new necklace and she bought himself a new watch.
4. Nick, Talia, and Miguel were classmates at the university. They haven't kept in touch with themselves until just recently.
5. Coach Haskins is forgetful. He often has to remind him to recharge his cell phone each night.
6. Dean talked to Brian and Hyung about Nick. He convinced themselves to avoid Nick until Nick could prove himself innocent.
7. Claire and Ryan, you've just finished a big project. Aren't you going to give yourself a break?
8. Nick is disappointed in him for being tricked. "How could I do this to myself?" he keeps asking.
9. We don't like to eat lunch by each other. Please join us.

Grammar 3

Modals of Possibility and Probability in the Past

Complete the sentences. Use expressions with must have, may have, might have, *or* could have *and the verb in parentheses. Sometimes more than 1 answer is possible.*

1. Tony **(be)** _____must have been_____ really busy today. He didn't even have time to eat lunch.

2. Amy **(enjoy)** _____ the movie. She decided to see it again.

3. Ms. Boyd **(not eat)** _____ anything at the party. She's a vegetarian and all the hors d'oeuvres were made with meat.

4. Talia **(not sleep)** _____ very well last night. She looks so sleepy this morning.

5. Dean and Jackie **(decide)** _____ to trick Nick a long time ago. Maybe they waited for just the right opportunity.

6. **Amy:** **(see)** _____ the receptionist _____ Jackie at The Gower Building?

   Talia: No, he **(not see)** _____ her. If he had seen her, he'd remember. He has a good memory.

7. For her birthday, Ms. Boyd's *Newsline* co-workers gave her a coffee cup and a pillow covered with pictures of cats. They **(know)** _____ she loves cats.

> **Study Tip**
> Try it out! Use new grammar points in your speech and writing. Keep track of which grammar points you use.

Language Functions

See Appendix 3 to review the language function charts.

Fill in the blanks in these conversations. Use the words in bold.

1. You met your friend for dinner and a movie. Now it's time to end the evening and say good-bye.

   You: **late / should** (*Make a closing comment; note the time.*)
   _____It's getting late. I really should be going._____

   Your friend: Yeah. I've got to go, too.

   You: **give** (*Invite the person to call you soon.*)

   _____

   Your friend: Sure, I'll do that.

   You: Great. See you later.

2. You ran into an old friend at a concert. You talked for a while, and now it's time to get back to your seat.

Your friend: Well, it was great seeing you.

You: **too** (*Return the same comment.*)

_____

     catch (*Confirm the next meeting: class tomorrow.*)

_____

3. You just saw a friend at the subway station and you chatted for a minute. Your friend is in a hurry because she has to run to her office.

You: **won't / your time** (*Make a closing comment.*)

_____

Your friend: OK. Well, it was great seeing you.

You: It was great seeing you, too.

     do this (*Suggest seeing each other again soon.*)

_____

Application Activities

1. **Listening and Speaking.** Keep a notebook of common expressions you hear in speech—from conversations around you, movies you watch, and so on. Include expressions for starting conversations and ending conversations. Find out the meaning of new expressions and try to use them in your own conversation.

2. **Grammar.** Think about an important personal event from your past. Write sentences with *must have, might have,* or *could have*. Why did it happen? How did people in the event feel? What could have happened differently?

3. **Writing.** Write 10 sentences about yourself and people you know. Use reflexive and reciprocal pronouns and other pronouns in your sentences. Here are some ideas: *give (someone) a break, remind . . . , be proud of . . . , be disappointed in . . . , encourage . . . , keep in touch with . . . .*

4. **Vocabulary.** Find at least 5 more food idioms (for example, *that's food for thought, you're the apple of my eye, my new car is a lemon*). Use a dictionary or ask a speaker of English to help you. Make categories to help you remember the meaning: a person (*a bad apple*), a thing (*a lemon*), an action. Compare your list of idioms with those of your classmates.

5. **Project.** Find out about a restaurant near you. You can use restaurant reviews from newspapers or tour guides, or you can consult websites for reviews. Find out about the food and the atmosphere of the restaurant. Write a short review or give a short presentation about the restaurant.

Grammar Explanations

This section contains the same grammar explanations that are found on the CD-ROM. They are included here for your quick reference. To view the animated presentation, go to the Grammar section of Unit A.4 in the CD-ROM course.

Grammar 1: Modals of Possibility and Probability

1. We use **modals of possibility** and **probability** to talk about things that we think are **possibly** or **probably true**.

   I **might** be a little late. If I am, please start without me.

   Valentino's **must** be a popular restaurant. It's sometimes hard to get a reservation.

2. *Must* expresses a **probability**. We use *must* when we're almost **100% sure** that something is **true**.

   Jackie: I've got to go. It **must** be time for my class.

   In the example, Jackie is almost sure that her class is ready to begin.

3. *May*, *might*, and *could* express a **possibility**. We use *may*, *might*, and *could* when we're less sure that something is true.

   Alicia: I don't think Professor Roberts is from the United States. I think he said he came here when he was a teenager.
   Anna: He **may** be Canadian.
   Toby: He **might** come from Australia.
   Dan: He **could** be British.

4. We use *can't* or *couldn't* when we are almost **100% sure** that something is **impossible**.

   Jackie: I'm sorry, but you **can't** be serious. I'm sure you're mistaken.

5. We use *must not* when we're a little less sure that something is impossible. We don't usually use a contraction with *must not*.

   Alicia: I heard that Nick Crawford is still trying to prove his innocence.
   Anna: He **must not** have any proof yet.

6. We use *may not* or *might not* when we think something is **impossible**, but we aren't very sure. We don't usually use a contraction with *may not* or *might not*.

   Jill: Crawford **may not** be innocent!
   Dan: Then again, he **might not** be guilty! We just don't know!

7. Remember, after a modal, you can only use the base form of the verb.

   Talia **must be** exhausted. She's working so hard.

8. In **questions**, we usually use *could*. We don't usually use *might, may,* or *must*.

   Alicia: What do you think? **Could** Crawford be guilty?

9. Notice that in **short answers** we usually use *be* if the question has a form of *be*.

   Alicia: What do you think? **Could** Crawford **be** guilty?
   Dan: Who knows? He **might be**.

   When a question has a verb other than *be*, we just use the modal in the short answer.

   Amy: **Could** Jackie really **have** an agent?
   Talia: She **could**. Anything's possible.

10. We can also use a verb like *think* to ask about possibility or probability. Notice that the reply still uses a modal.

    Alicia: **Do** you **think** Crawford is guilty?
    Dan: He **might** be.

Grammar 2: Reflexive and Reciprocal Pronouns

1. We use **reflexive pronouns** when the subject and the object of a sentence refer to **the same person**.

   Talia: **You** should be proud of **yourself**, Amy.

   In this sentence the **subject** (*You*) is Amy. The **object** (*yourself*) is also Amy. The subject and the object are the same person: Amy. So, Amy should be proud of Amy. In other words, Amy should be proud of herself.

2. These are the reflexive pronouns: *myself, yourself, himself, herself, itself, ourselves, yourselves,* and *themselves*.

Reflexive Pronouns
I looked at **myself** in the mirror.
You looked at **yourself** in the mirror.
He looked at **himself** in the mirror.
She looked at **herself** in the mirror.
It looked at **itself** in the mirror.
We looked at **ourselves** in the mirror.
You looked at **yourselves** in the mirror.
They looked at **themselves** in the mirror.

Modals of Possibility and Probability		
100% sure		
Affirmative	↑	**Negative**
must		can't, couldn't
could, may, might		must not
	↓	may not, might not
less sure		

3. Notice that **you** has 2 reflexive pronouns. Use **yourself** when you're speaking to 1 person. Use **yourselves** when you're speaking to more than 1 person.

> **Tony:** Take care of **yourself**, Talia.
> **Talia:** I will.
>
> **Tony:** Take care of **yourselves**, guys.
> **Talia and Amy:** We will.

4. We can also use a **reciprocal pronoun** (**each other** or **one another**) when the subject and object of a sentence are the same people. But in this case, the people have a **2-way**, or reciprocal, relationship.

> **Talia and Jackie** are talking to **each other**.

In this sentence the subject is *Talia and Jackie*. The object (*each other*) is also Talia and Jackie. The subject and the object are the same 2 people: Talia and Jackie. The sentence means that Talia is talking to Jackie and that Jackie is talking to Talia. They are having a 2-way conversation.

Notice that the sentence *Talia and Jackie are talking to themselves* has a very different meaning. This means that Talia is talking to herself and Jackie is talking to herself. They are not having a 2-way conversation.

5. We usually use **each other** when the subject is **2 people**.

> **Talia and Amy** know **each other** from work.

We use **each other** or **one another** when the subject is **more than 2 people**.

> **Talia, Amy, and Tony** know **each other** from work.
> **Talia, Amy, and Tony** know **one another** from work.

Grammar 3: Modals of Possibility and Probability in the Past

1. We use **modals of possibility and probability in the past** to talk about things that **possibly or probably happened**. We form these modals with **modal** + **have** + the **past participle of the verb**.

> **Tony:** Amy did great work. She **must have been** proud of herself.

2. *Must have* expresses **probability**. We use **must have** or the contraction **must've** when we're almost 100% sure that something was true.

> **Talia:** I **must have left** my briefcase in the office. I'm almost certain that's where it is.

3. *May have, might have,* and *could have* express **possibility**. We use **may have, might have,** or **could have** (or the contractions **may've, might've,** or **could've**) when we're less sure that something was true.

> **Jackie:** We **might have seen** each other around campus.
> **Talia:** Or we **may have been** in a class together.
> **Jackie:** Yeah. It **could have been** last semester.

4. We use **can't have** or **couldn't have** when we're almost 100% sure that something was impossible.

> **Jackie:** It **couldn't have been** in a journalism class. I'm taking acting classes.

5. We use **must not have** when we are a little less sure that something was impossible. We don't usually use a contraction with **must not**.

> **Amy:** She left in a big hurry. She **must not have wanted** to be late for class.

6. We use **may not have** or **might not have** when we think something was impossible but we aren't very sure. We don't usually use a contraction with **may not** or **might not**.

> **Talia:** She **may not have wanted** to talk to me anymore.

Modals of Possibility and Probability in the Past

100% sure

Affirmative	Negative
must have	can't have, couldn't have
could have, may have, might have	must not have may not have, might not have

less sure

---

7. In **questions**, we use **could have**. We don't use *may have, might have,* or *must have*.

> **Talia:** **Could** she **have been** at the soccer game?

8. Notice that in **short answers**, we use *been* if the question has a form of *be*.

> **Talia:** **Could** he **have been** the star?
> **Amy:** He **could have been**.

When a question has a verb other than *be*, we use the modal plus *have*.

> **Talia:** **Could** she **have seen** us there?
> **Amy:** She **could have**.

9. We can also use a verb without a modal to ask about possibility or probability.

> **Talia:** **Was** she at the soccer game?
> **Amy:** She **could have been**.

B.1 | Talia's Brilliant Plan

Listening

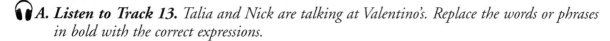

🎧 **A. Listen to Track 13.** *Talia and Nick are talking at Valentino's. Replace the words or phrases in bold with the correct expressions.*

Talia: Oh, thank goodness you got my message.

Nick: Yeah. What's going on?

Talia: Don't worry. I'm not trying to (1) ~~make you take me~~ *get you to take me out* **out** on a date. I'm trying to (2) **get you to save** your career.

Nick: Oh, that. Yeah, right, I almost forgot.

Talia: Be serious. I care about . . . I care about your future.

Nick: (3) **I do, too!**

Talia: Good—you wore a tie.

Nick: Yeah, your message said, wear a tie and a jacket. You look nice, by the way.

Talia: Thanks. (4) **You do, too**. . . . So, as I was saying, I have a feeling Dean and Jackie (5) **are planning to talk about** you as soon as they get here.

🎧 **B. Listen to Track 14.** *You will hear an excerpt from a lecture on warning signals. Complete the summary. Use the words in the box.*

siren	cough	freeze	thinking	seek	alarm

All of us respond to warning sounds quite naturally without (1)_____. Our natural response to any warning sound is a feeling of (2) "_____." Low-frequency warning sounds, like a (3)_____, cause us to (4) "_____," that is, to bring ourselves to a complete stop. High-frequency warning sounds, like a (5)_____, warn us to (6) "_____" something. We will generally look around, to see what the cause of the alarm is.

Vocabulary

See Appendix 2 to review the vocabulary terms.

A. Look at each word in the box. Is it an adjective or a noun? Fill in the chart.

bald	braid	cornrows	crew cut	curly
kinky	ponytail	straight	wavy	wig

Adjective	Noun		
	One-word noun		Two-word noun
	Noun	*Compound noun*	
1. bald	6.	8.	10.
2.	7.	9.	
3.			
4.			
5.			

B. Jackie has volunteered to introduce the models at a fashion show. Read her script and use the vocabulary words to summarize the description.

Model 1's hair *has loose curls*, and it is *pulled behind her head and tied*.

She has (1) (*adj*) _____ hair, and it is pulled back into a (2) (*n*) _____.

Model 2's hair has been designed in *small, tight braids along her head*. I imagine that when she undoes the braids, her hair will have *lots of curls*!

She has (3) (*n*) _____ in her hair. Jackie thinks her hair will be (4) (*adj*) _____ when she undoes her hair.

Model 3 is displaying a popular summer idea—*very short hair*. In fact, it almost looks as if he *has no hair*!

He has a (5) (*n*) _____, and he almost looks (6) (*adj*) _____.

Model 4 has styled her long hair *without curls* by *separating it into 3 pieces and weaving them together*. It looks beautiful.

She has long (7) (*adj*) _____ hair, made into a (8) (*n*) _____.

Model 5 has *a lot of tight curls*. It almost looks as if it's not her real hair, but a *covering of hair* instead!

She has (9) (*adj*) _____ hair, and it looks as if she's wearing a (10) (*n*) _____.

Grammar 1

Make, Have, Get, Let, and Help

A. *Choose the best verb from the first pair to complete each sentence. Be sure to adjust the verb form if necessary. Then put the second verb into the correct form.*

1. **Ms. Boyd:** I (**help / make**) ____helped____ John Donnelly (**become**) ____become____ a great reporter. I gave him lots of expert tips!

2. **Casting director:** I (**not let / let**) _____ Jackie (**have**) _____ a small part in the play. She didn't stop crying until I finally said, "OK."

3. **Jackie:** The writer of the play (**have / make**) _____ his secretary (**send**) _____ me a copy of the script. The writer was hoping I would agree to play the main character.

4. **Jackie:** I can (**get / let**) _____ any director (**hire**) _____ me. All I have to do is walk into a room, and they forget about all the other actors!

5. **Nick:** I had plans to go a party tonight, but Talia (**make / let**) _____ me (**cancel**) _____ them so she and I could meet at Valentino's. She said it was urgent.

6. **Talia:** I don't like working with John. He (**not make / not let**) _____ me (**do**) _____ anything by myself.

B. *Read each statement, paying special attention to the phrases in bold. What is the speaker thinking? Think about the verbs* (make, have, get, let, help). *Circle all the things that you can infer—or guess—that the speaker is thinking.*

1. **Talia:** Tony **is making me** work with John on this report.

   (A.) Talia probably wants to do the report herself or doesn't want to work with John for some other reason.

   B. Talia probably asked Tony if she could work with John.

   C. Talia is happy that she is working with John.

   (D.) Talia is working with John only because her boss wants her to.

2. **Claire:** Tony **let me do** some extra work! I **got him to give me** the Truman report.

   A. Claire appreciates Tony's assignment.

   B. Claire probably would have preferred a break.

   C. Claire probably asked Tony to give her the extra work.

   D. Tony wanted to give Claire the extra work.

3. **Talia:** Amy **got me to wear** this dress to Valentino's tonight.

   A. Amy probably insisted that Talia wear a certain dress because she wants her to look good.

   B. Talia probably asked to borrow Amy's dress and Amy didn't want to lend it to her.

   C. Talia may be a little annoyed at Amy for her "help," but she probably isn't very angry.

   D. Talia could have said "no" to Amy, but she let Amy make the decision for her.

Grammar 2

Study Tip
Volunteer! Say 3 things in class every day. Ask questions.

So and Neither

The staff at Newsline *is having a costume party; everyone is dressed up. Fill in each blank with an expression using* so *or* neither, *using the cues in parentheses when needed.*

1. **Amy:**   Oh, look! There's Jeremy in the Spiderman costume. Isn't he cute?!

   Talia: Yeah. And (**his wife**) _____ so is his wife _____. She's dressed up as Spiderman's friend Mary Jane.

2. **Talia:**   Is that Ryan with the dark wig and glasses?

   Amy: I can't tell who that is.

   Claire: (**I**) _____. Who is he?

3. **John:**   Have Kim and Alex arrived yet?

   Claire: No, not yet. And (**Tad and Ryan**) _____. They'll be here around 10:00.

4. **Amy:**   I love your costume, Tony.

   Talia: (**I**) _____. You look really good as James Bond!

5. **Jorge:**   Hey, Spiderman! What a great costume!

   Jeremy: Thanks, but I didn't really want be Spiderman. My wife chose my costume for me.

   Jorge: (**mine**) _____. You didn't think it was my idea to dress as a giant banana, did you?!

6. **Talia:**   You did a great job with these crab cakes, John. They're delicious!

   John: Thanks. I'm glad you like them. Would you like another?

   Talia: I'd love one.

   Jeremy: (**I**) _____.

Future Time Clauses

Amy is taking a screenwriting class. Her assignment is to present an idea for a spy movie. Read her script outline. Correct the errors in bold in the outline.

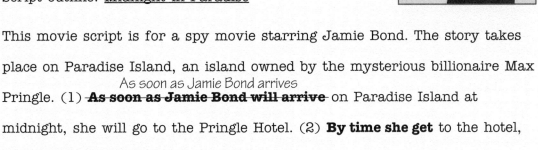

English 201: Screenwriting   Amy Lee

Script outline: <u>Midnight in Paradise</u>

This movie script is for a spy movie starring Jamie Bond. The story takes place on Paradise Island, an island owned by the mysterious billionaire Max Pringle. (1) ~~**As soon as Jamie Bond will arrive**~~ *As soon as Jamie Bond arrives* on Paradise Island at midnight, she will go to the Pringle Hotel. (2) **By time she get** to the hotel, (3) **a large party will taking place**.

(4) **After Jamie will put on** a disguise, she will enter the hotel ballroom.

(5) **While Jamie be** in the ballroom, she will talk to the other guests. She will want to find out the location of Max Pringle's private safe, which contains secret documents. (6) **When she will finding** the location of the hidden safe, she will open it with her laser-beam lipstick case.

After she opens the safe, (7) **she is going to be taking** photographs of the documents with her mini-camera. Alarms will go off (8) **as soon as she will open** the safe. She will have only 30 seconds (9) **before Pringle's security guards are arriving**. Bond will continue to take photographs (10) **until the guards entered the room**.

(11) **After Jamie has left** the hotel, she will jump off a high cliff into the ocean. By the time she hits the water, (12) **a helicopter will waiting** to pick her up.

Language Functions

See Appendix 3 to review the language function charts.

Jackie's family is complimenting her on a performance. Give paraphrases. Use the words in bold.

1. **Jackie's father:** Great job! I'd like to compliment you on your performance. I really enjoyed it!

   Jackie: Thanks for the compliment.

   What else could Jackie say? **(nice of you)**

   That's nice of you to say.
   _____

2. **Jackie's mother:** You looked great on stage! And the play went really well.

   Jackie: Thanks. I tried really hard on stage to do well.

   What else could Jackie say? **(my best)**

   _____

3. **Jackie's grandmother:** Honey, way to go! I thought you acted very well on stage.

   Jackie: Thanks, Grandma. I appreciate it.

   What else could Jackie's grandmother say? **(great actress)**

   _____

Application Activities

1. **Grammar.** Write about someone who has guided you in your life. For example, maybe a teacher helped you understand something important, or a relative let you do something exciting, or a friend got you to start a new job. Use *help, make, let*, and *get* in your paragraph.

2. **Vocabulary.** Look through an entertainment magazine. Try to describe the hair of several people. Find as many words as you can to describe hair (texture, color, style, or products associated with hair) and clothes.

3. **Speaking.** Give compliments to at least 3 different people this week. Note how these people respond to your compliment. What expressions did they use? Did they accept it, downplay it, or offer you a compliment in return?

4. **Project.** Watch a spy movie such as a James Bond movie, *Austin Powers, Spy Kids*, or another kind of movie with special gadgets such as *Batman*. Make notes on the amazing futuristic devices the characters use in the movie. Describe them to the class or write a short description of them.

Grammar Explanations

This section contains the same grammar explanations that are found on the CD-ROM. They are included here for your quick reference. To view the animated presentation, go to the Grammar section of Unit B.1 in the CD-ROM course.

Grammar 1: *Make, Have, Get, Let,* and *Help*

1. We use *make* + an object + the base form of the verb to talk about when a person **forces** another person to do something.
   > **Nick:** Are you really going to make me put these on?
   > **Talia:** Yes.

2. We use *have* + an object + the base form of the verb to talk about when a person **causes** another person to do something. *Have* is not as strong as *make*.
   > Talia **had Amy call** Valentino's to make reservations.

3. We use *get* to talk about when a person **persuades** another person to do something. Notice that *get* is followed by an object + an infinitive—not the base form.
   > **Talia:** I'm not trying to get you to take me out on a date.

   We do **NOT** say: ~~I'm not trying to get you take me out.~~

4. We use *let* + an object + the base form to talk about when a person **permits** another person to do something.
   > Tony **let Talia work** on the Crawford story.

5. We can use *help* + an object + the base form of the verb or the infinitive.
   > **Talia:** I'm trying to help you save your career.
   > I'm trying to help you to save your career.

   These 2 sentences have the same meaning, but *help* + the base form is more common.

Grammar 2: *So* and *Neither*

1. We often use short sentences with *so* to express agreement with another speaker. When we use this type of response, we don't have to repeat the information in the first statement.
   > **Talia:** I care about your future.
   > **Nick:** So do I!

   Here, *So do I* means *I care about my future, too.*

   We can also use *so* and *neither* to add similar information to what another speaker has said.
   > **Nick:** Jackie doesn't look very happy.
   > **Talia:** **Neither** does Dean.

   In the example, *Neither does Dean* means *Dean doesn't look very happy, either.*

2. We use short sentences with *so* to respond to an affirmative statement. We form the response with *so* + a form of *be* or an auxiliary verb + the subject.
   > **Nick:** The fish is delicious.
   > **Talia:** **So is the chicken.**

In the example, *So is the chicken* means *The chicken is delicious, too.*
   > **Nick:** You look nice.
   > **Talia:** **So do you.**

In the example, *So do you* means *You look nice, too.*

Notice that the verb comes before the subject.

We do **NOT** say: ~~So the chicken is.~~

3. We use short sentences with *neither* to respond to a **negative** statement.
   > **Nick:** I'm not really hungry.
   > **Talia:** **Neither am I.**

   > **Nick:** Dean hasn't noticed us.
   > **Talia:** **Neither has Jackie.**

Notice that the verb comes before the subject.

We do **NOT** say: ~~Neither Jackie has.~~

4. The response always uses a form of *be* or an **auxiliary** verb (*be, have, do,* or a modal such as *can, could, should, would*).

   If the statement has a form of *be* or an auxiliary verb, use a form of *be* or the same auxiliary verb in the response.
   > **Talia:** I'm nervous.
   > **Nick:** So **am** I.

   > **Nick:** I've never been to Valentino's.
   > **Talia:** Neither **have** I.

   > **Talia:** This pasta **is** delicious.
   > **Nick:** So **are** the vegetables.

5. If the statement doesn't have a form of *be* or an auxiliary verb, use a form of *do* in the response. Use the **same tense** as the verb in the statement.
   > Nick **plays** soccer.
   > So **does** Dean.

   > Talia **went** to college.
   > So **did** Nick.

So and *Neither*	
Statement	**Response**
affirmative	with *so*
negative	with *neither*
a form of *be*	a form of *be*
don't or *doesn't*	*do* or *does*
a verb without auxiliary	a form of *do*
same tense as in response	same tense as in statement
subject + verb	verb + subject

Grammar 3: Future Time Clauses

1. We often use a **future time clause** with a **main clause** to show the relationship between 2 future events. They show which event will happen first and which will happen next.

> **Talia: Dean and Jackie are going to talk about you as soon as they get here.**

In the example, *Dean and Jackie are going to talk about you* is the **main clause**. *As soon as they get here* is the **future time clause**.

Talia means that first, Dean and Jackie will get to the restaurant. Immediately after that, they'll talk about Nick.

2. The verb in the **main clause** is in the **future** with *will* or *be going to*. The verb in the **time clause** is in the **present.**

> **Nick: I'll cough when I see them.**

I'll cough is the **main clause**. *When I see them* is the **future time clause**.

Remember, we don't use *will* or *be going to* in a future time clause.

We do **NOT** say: ~~I'll cough when I'll see them~~.

3. We often use *when*, *after*, and *as soon as* in a future time clause to introduce the event that will happen first.

> Nick and Talia will go into Valentino's **as soon as they put on their wigs.**

In the example, Nick and Talia will first put on their wigs. Then they will go into Valentino's.

4. We often use *before*, *until*, and *by the time* in a future time clause to introduce the event that will happen second.

> Talia and Nick will get the proof they need **before they finish dinner.**

In the example, Nick and Talia will get the proof. Then they will finish dinner.

5. We use *while* in a future time clause to introduce an event that will happen at the same time as another event.

> **While Dean and Jackie talk, Nick and Talia will listen** to their conversation.

In the example, Dean and Jackie will talk. At the same time, Nick and Talia will listen.

6. The **future time clause** can come at the **beginning or end** of the sentence. The meaning does not change. When the future time clause comes at the beginning of the sentence, we use a comma after it.

> **Nick: While you plant the mike, I'll look out for Dean and Jackie.**
> **I'll look out for Dean and Jackie while you plant the mike.**

Both sentences have the same meaning.

B.2 Dean's Double Cross

Listening

🎧 **A. Listen to Track 15.** *Jackie and Dean are talking over dinner at Valentino's. Fill in the blanks in the conversation.*

Jackie: So this woman—Amy—and I

(1)_____ when a friend of hers

(2)_____. Then, when Amy

introduced us, her friend said I looked familiar.

Dean: So?

Jackie: So then she asked me (3)_____

for Kicks Shoes!

Dean: There is no Kicks Shoes.

Jackie: I know that, and you know that, but she doesn't . . .

Dean: (4)_____ about . . .

Jackie: I'm scared, Dean. She works for *Newsline*.

🎧 **B. Listen to Track 16.** *Jackie and Dean are arguing in the restaurant. Fill in the blanks in the conversation.*

Jackie: . . . when are you going to introduce me to Byron Walters?

Dean: Byron Walters?

Jackie: Yes, that film director friend of yours? Remember? The director

(1)_____ a star!!

Dean: Oh, him . . .

Jackie: You said (2)_____, but this is getting ridiculous.

Dean: Uh, I forgot to tell you. There is no Byron Walters. He quit the business.

Jackie: But (3)_____ my big break, the break that's going to make me

a star.

🎧 C. **Listen to Track 17.** *Selena is telling the story of how she met Robert. Read each statement and write* **T** *(True),* **F** *(False), or* **NI** *(no information, not in the story).*

_____ 1. Selena and Robert both know a man named Bassam.

_____ 2. Robert and Selena met for the first time at Bassam's party.

_____ 3. Robert and Selena are both from Michigan.

_____ 4. Selena and Robert went to the same high school.

_____ 5. Robert played baseball in high school.

_____ 6. Robert is several years older than Selena.

_____ 7. Selena was on the soccer team at her high school.

_____ 8. Selena used to have short hair when she was in high school.

_____ 9. Robert and Selena weren't attracted to each other when they first met.

_____ 10. Robert and Selena are planning to get married.

Vocabulary

See Appendix 2 to review the vocabulary terms.

Read each situation. Fill in the blanks with an expression using keep.

1. Can you tell me what happened? Please don't _____keep_____ me _____guessing_____! I don't want to be kept in the dark any longer!

2. Please stop asking so many questions. _____ your _____! I'll give you a full report tomorrow morning.

3. Will you _____ to _____? You're talking about too many different things. I can't keep up with you!

4. It's so noisy in this dorm. Hey! Would you guys _____? I'm trying to study.

5. Aunt Ruth is in the hospital, so I'm going to visit her. I'll _____, OK? I'll give you a call next Friday and let you know how she's doing.

6. Margie and Ellen are arguing again. I don't want to get involved in their argument. Please _____ me _____ it!

Simple Past with *When* and Past Continuous with *When*

A. *Read each sentence. Then write* **T** *(True) or* **F** *(False) next to each idea. Both ideas may be true or both ideas may be false.*

1. When I saw Talia, she was talking with Nick.

    __T__ Talia was talking with Nick. Then I saw her.

    __F__ I saw Talia. Then she started talking with Nick.

2. When Nick arrived at the restaurant, Talia was waiting for him.

    ____ Talia arrived at the restaurant first.

    ____ Nick arrived at the restaurant after Talia.

3. When Dean came into the restaurant, Nick and Talia were sitting at their table.

    ____ Nick and Talia arrived at the restaurant before Dean.

    ____ Nick, Talia, and Dean came into the restaurant at the same time.

4. Dean looked very surprised when Jackie told him about Talia.

    ____ After Jackie told Dean about Talia, Dean became very surprised.

    ____ Dean was surprised about Talia before Jackie talked to him.

5. When Jackie got angry, she stormed out of the restaurant.

    ____ Jackie became angry after she left the restaurant.

    ____ Jackie left the restaurant because she got angry.

B. *Rewrite each pair of sentences as a single sentence. Use* when. *There are usually two acceptable ways to write each* when *sentence.*

1. First Jackie mentioned her meeting with Talia. Then Dean got upset.

    When Jackie mentioned her meeting with Talia, Dean got upset.

    OR Dean got upset when Jackie mentioned her meeting with Talia.

2. First Nick saw Dean. Then he coughed to warn Talia.

    _____

3. First Jackie sat down. Then Dean asked Jackie why she didn't answer her phone.

    _____

4. First Dean kept interrupting Jackie. Then Jackie became very angry.

    _____

5. First Dean told Jackie about Byron Walters. Then Jackie threatened Dean.

    _____

Grammar 2

Reported Imperatives

A. *Read each imperative sentence. Then rewrite it as a reported imperative.*

1. Dean (*to his dog, Kicker*): Sit!

(command) ___Dean commanded Kicker to sit.___

2. Nick (*to Brian*): Don't go to Valentino's. The prices are too high.

(advise) ___Nick advised Brian not to go to Valentino's because the prices are too high.___

3. Talia (*to Claire*): Don't drink that milk! It's sour.

(warn) _____

4. Dean (*to Nick*): Prove that I framed you!

(challenge) _____

5. Tony (*to his research staff*): Remember to hand in your background research by the end of the day. And that means *everyone*!

(remind) _____

6. Dean (*to his dog, Kicker*): Don't chew on my new shoes!

(tell) _____

7. Amy (*to Talia*): Come watch a movie with Josh and me at my apartment tomorrow night.

(invite) _____

8. Jackie (*to a classmate*): Don't be late again! Dr. Roberts doesn't tolerate lateness.

(warn) _____

B. *Write 2 sentences about things your boss, your parents, your teacher, or your friends told you to do or not do. Write each sentence 2 ways, once with* tell *and once with* say.

EXAMPLE: ___My parents told me to be careful when I travel abroad.___

___My parents said to be careful when I travel abroad.___

1. _____

_____

2. _____

_____

Grammar 3

Subject Adjective Clauses

A. *Combine the 2 sentences into 1 sentence using a subject adjective clause.*

1. Ming Wu is an artist. He painted a portrait of Jackie.

   Ming Wu is the artist who painted a portrait of Jackie.

2. "Angel-Napped" is a *Newsline* story. It's about a kidnapped baby.

   _____

3. Wraps is a small company. It's owned by Talia's friend Mandy.

   _____

4. Aron is a chef. He works at a restaurant called Prima.

   _____

5. Tuffy is one of Amy's cats. It used to be very shy when Amy first adopted it.

   _____

B. *Finish the sentences with your own words by adding adjective clauses that modify the given subjects.*

1. **Yumiko:** Which soccer player is Nick Crawford?

   Jessie: (*Nick is being investigated by the Soccer Federation.*) Oh, yeah! He's the soccer player

   who's _____ _being investigated by the Soccer Federation_ _____.

2. **Joe:** Dean Bishop? Is he the soccer player who supposedly took a bribe?

   Freddie: No. You're thinking of Nick Crawford. (*Dean is jealous of Nick Crawford.*) Dean is the

   one _____.

3. **Ricardo:** Which one of those teachers is Ms. Davis?

   Georgia: (*Ms. Davis is wearing a blue sweater.*) Ms. Davis is the person _____

   _____.

4. **Greg:** Do you know Talia and Amy? What do they do?

   Marisa: (*Talia and Amy work in the news division at* Newsline.) Talia and Amy? Sure. They're

   the ones _____.

5. **Your friend:** I've heard of the movie (*name a movie*) _____, but I can't remember

   anything about it.

   You: (*Give any information about the movie.*) I know that movie! It's the movie _____

   _____.

6. Your family member: Do you know anything about (*name a sport, animal, plant, or other*

topic) _____?

You: (*Give some information about the sport, animal, plant, or other topic.*) A little.

It's the _____

_____.

Language Functions

See Appendix 3 to review the language function charts.

Complete the conversations. Fill in the blanks with appropriate phrases from the language function charts. Use the cues in parentheses.

Talia: June Mattox is a better actress than Naomi Harris. June Mattox has much more talent . . .

Amy: No, I don't think so. Naomi Harris is clearly better.

Talia: (1) (*asks Amy not to interrupt*) _____. June Mattox is much more emotional
in her roles. And she was in my favorite movie, *The Last Dance.*

Amy: No. You're wrong about that. June Mattox wasn't in *The Last Dance.* She was in *The First Kiss.*

Talia: Oh. (2) (*concedes to Amy*) _____. I can't quite remember.

Amy: Oh, well, it doesn't really matter. Do you want to go see a movie?

Nick: So I think Quick Burger has the best burgers. They're the biggest burger for the lowest price,
and they . . .

Billy: No, (3) (*disagrees with Nick*) _____. Meat House has the cheapest prices
in town!

Nick: (4) (*asks Billy not to interrupt*) _____? What I meant was that you can get
the best deal at Quick Burger: They have the biggest burger, and the price is good for the size.

Billy: Oh. (5) (*concedes to Nick*) _____. I suppose that's true.

Nick: So. Do you want to go get a burger?

Application Activities

Study Tip
Write summaries of the CD-ROM video story for extra practice each week.

1. **Grammar.** Write at least 5 sentences about your family, your classmates, or your co-workers. Identify the people in the group by using subject adjective clauses to describe them. For example, *Claudia is my older sister. She's the member of my family who . . .*

2. **Vocabulary.** Write at least 5 sentences using the *keep* expressions from this unit. Think of specific people you would like to say these sentences to. Give a specific situation if possible. For example: *To my friend Carol when she's telling me to hurry up:* <u>*Keep your shirt on*</u>, *Carol! I'm almost ready to go. To the waiter at the café I go to every day: Thanks.* <u>*Keep the change*</u>*. See you tomorrow.*

3. **Listening.** Watch a TV political debate show or watch a movie review show with more than 1 critic. Listen for the main ideas and watch for specific expressions and body language that are used to signal disagreement. Make a sketch of at least 5 gestures. What does each gesture show?

4. **Discussion.** Choose a current topic from the news. Start a conversation with several people this week. Give your opinion of the topic and ask others to give theirs. Try to use some new expressions to show polite disagreement.

5. **Project.** The reading topic in this unit is stress. Design a short questionnaire about stress. Ask any questions you like, such as *How stressed out are you? What stresses you out the most?* Use a variety of question types like multiple choice, true / false, and open-ended questions. Give your survey to at least 5 different people. Report the results to the class.

Grammar Explanations

This section contains the same grammar explanations that are found on the CD-ROM. They are included here for your quick reference. To view the animated presentation, go to the Grammar section of Unit B.2 in the CD-ROM course.

Grammar 1: Simple Past with *When* and Past Continuous with *When*

1. We use the **past continuous** to talk about an action that was in progress at a specific time in the past. When we use the past continuous, we aren't interested in when the activity ended.
   Jackie: It was 6:00. I **was sitting** in the student lounge.

   We use the **simple past** to talk about another action that **interrupts** that action.
   Jackie: I **was sitting** in the student lounge when a woman **came up** to me.

   In the example, first Jackie sat down in the student lounge. Then a woman came up to her.

   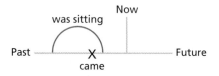

2. We use **when** to introduce the **simple past** action.
   Jackie: Amy and I **were talking when** a friend of hers **showed up**.

   In this example, first Amy and Jackie started talking. Then Amy's friend showed up.

3. When both clauses are in the simple past, the meaning is very different. Notice the difference in these 2 examples.
   When Jackie **arrived** at Valentino's, Nick and Talia **looked** at their menus.

   In this example, first Jackie arrived at Valentino's. Then Nick and Talia looked at their menus.
   When Jackie **arrived at** Valentino's, Nick and Talia **were looking** at their menus.

   In this example, Nick and Talia were looking at their menus. Then Jackie arrived at Valentino's.

4. The part of the sentence that begins with **when** is called a **time clause**. The time clause can come at the beginning or the end of the sentence. The meaning is the same.
   When Jackie asked about Byron Walters, Dean seemed surprised.
   Dean seemed surprised **when Jackie asked about Byron Walters.**

   When the time clause comes first, we put a **comma** after it. When the main clause comes first, we don't use a comma between the 2 clauses.

Grammar 2: Reported Imperatives

1. We use **imperatives**, such as *Be quiet*, to give commands, make suggestions, give directions, and extend invitations. A **direct imperative** uses the person's exact words.
   Dean said, **"Be quiet!"**

   When we write, we put **quotation marks** around direct imperatives.

2. We can also report imperatives without using the person's exact words. In this case, we use **reported imperatives**.
   Dean told Jackie **to be quiet.**

   When we write, we don't use quotation marks around reported imperatives.

   We do **NOT** write: ~~Dean told Jackie "to be quiet."~~

3. The most common **reporting verbs** are *say* and *tell*.
   We use *say* when we don't mention the listener.
   Dean **said** to be quiet.

   We do **NOT** say: ~~Dean said Jackie to be quiet.~~

   We use *tell* when we mention the listener.
   Dean **told Jackie** to be quiet.
   He **told her** to be quiet.

   We do **NOT** say: ~~Dean told to be quiet.~~

4. To report an **affirmative imperative**, use the infinitive.
   Dean: Keep your voice down!
   OR I told you **to keep** your voice down.

5. To report a **negative imperative**, use *not* + the infinitive.
   Jackie: Don't interrupt!
   I told you **not to interrupt**!

6. In reported imperatives, we sometimes have to **change pronouns** to keep the original meaning.
   Talia: Amy, call me later.
   John: Talia told Amy to call **her** later.

7. We sometimes have to change **time phrases** to keep the original meaning.
   Talia: Call me **tomorrow**, Amy.
   Alicia: Talia told Amy to call her **the next day**.

Grammar 3: Subject Adjective Clauses

1. **Adjective clauses** (also caused **relative clauses**) identify nouns or indefinite pronouns such as *one, someone,* and *something.*

    Jackie: You're the **one who got me into this**, Dean.

    Who got me into this is an adjective clause. It identifies Dean. In other words, Dean got Jackie into the situation.

2. Adjective clauses begin with a **relative pronoun**. We can use the relative pronoun **who** or **that** when the subject of the adjective clause is a **person**.

    Dean: I was the **guy who sent the phony tape to** *Newsline.*

    I was the **guy that sent the phony tape to** *Newsline.*

    We use the **relative pronoun** *that* or *which* when the subject is a **place** or **thing**.

    Jackie: That was the **break that was going to make me a star.**

    That was the **break which was going to make me a star.**

    Lisa: Don't you work in the Gower Building?

    Ben: No. I work in the **building that's across from the Gower Building.**

    I work in the **building which is across from the Gower Building.**

    That is more common than *which* in informal conversation.

3. The relative pronoun combines 2 sentences into one sentence.

    Talia's the reporter. She's covering the story.
    Talia's the reporter **who's covering the story.**

    This is the story. It's airing tonight.
    This is the story **that's airing tonight.**

4. Relative pronouns **don't change forms**. They're the same for singular and plural subjects. They are also the same for male and female subjects.

    That's the **man who** works at *Newsline.*
    Those are the **women who** work at *Newsline.*

5. Notice that the **verb in the adjective clause** is singular if it refers to a singular subject.

    That's the **reporter** who **works** for *Newsline.*

    The verb is plural if it refers to a plural subject.

    Those are the **reporters** who **work** for *Newsline.*

B.3 | Another Confession

A. Listen to Track 18. *Nick and Talia are talking in the restaurant. Match the beginnings and endings of the sentences.*

__d__	**1. Nick:** How did you know	**a.** we'll still be able to catch Tony.
_____	**2. Talia:** I knew she would tell Dean about it	**b.** we were studying together in the library . . .
_____	**3. Nick:** I was beginning	**c.** by mid-semester.
_____	**4. Talia:** Are you ready	**d.** they were going to talk about me?
_____	**5. Talia:** If we leave now,	**e.** to enjoy ourselves?
_____	**6. Nick:** Why don't we just take a little time now	**f.** as soon as she could.
_____	**7. Nick:** I have a confession	**g.** but we split up during that semester.
_____	**8. Nick:** And do you remember when	**h.** to think it was all over for me.
_____	**9. Talia:** I had a boyfriend,	**i.** to make.
_____	**10. Talia:** In fact, we had split up	**j.** to go?

B. Listen to Track 19. *You will hear an excerpt from a lecture about memory. Complete the ideas from the lecture. Use the words in the box.*

imagination	combination	emotions
images	change	influenced

1. Our memories are a _____ of several mental processes.

2. Our memories are constructed out of _____ from the original event, plus our _____, beliefs, _____, dreams, and the many things we have heard or read.

3. Our memories _____ over time.

4. Our memories are _____ by the situation and the people around us.

Vocabulary

See Appendix 2 to review the vocabulary terms.

ask someone out	fix somebody up	play the field
be in a serious relationship	be on the rebound	split up
have a crush on somebody	go on a blind date	play hard to get
be seeing somebody		

Read these sections from an advice column by Dr. Love. Replace the phrases in bold with expressions from the box. Use the correct form.

Be clear!

have a crush on somebody

If you (1) **really like someone**, don't be shy about it. Tell the person how you feel. Then (2) **invite him or her to go somewhere together**! You'll never know how that person will respond until you ask. Just get out there and give it a try!

If someone asks you out, be honest. If you're already (3) **in a romantic relationship with someone**, it's important to say that. It's not right (4) **to make it difficult for the person to start a relationship with you**. If you're interested, say yes. If you're not, say no. (But do it politely!)

Beware . . . !

Ladies, this tip is for you. Beware of guys who (5) **are having more than one romantic relationship at the same time**. There are many men who want lots of short-term relationships. Also beware of men who have just (6) **ended a serious relationship** with another woman and (7) **are still upset by the end of the relationship**. If you want to (8) **be with someone for a long time**, these are probably not the men you should date.

Just ask!

If you are having trouble meeting that "special someone," talk to your friends. Ask if they can introduce you to someone. Maybe they can (9) **find someone who might be suitable for you** or arrange for you to (10) **meet and go out for the first time**. Who knows? It may just work out!

Future Conditional

Talia and Amy are listening to Dr. Love's radio advice show. Fill in each blank with the future (will *or* be going to) *or simple present form of the verb in parentheses. Use a modal* (might, may, *or* can) *where appropriate.*

Caller 1: Hi, my name is Natalie. I have a crush on a co-worker. We talk a little bit during our lunch break, but I've never had the courage to tell him how I feel. Dr. Love, I don't know what to do. Is it OK for a girl to ask a guy out?

1. If you (**not tell**) _____don't tell_____ him your true feelings, you (**regret**) _____'ll regret_____ it. You may lose your chance forever.

2. It's OK for a girl to ask a guy out in today's society. He (**probably feel**) _____ thrilled if you (**ask him out**) _____.

3. On the other hand, if you (**date**) _____ him and the two of you (**split up**) _____, you (**have**) _____ difficulty working together in the same office.

Caller 2: Hi, my name is Philip. There's a girl in my college dorm I'm really interested in, but I've never even spoken to her. I've been following her around campus and trying to learn more about her. What should I do now?

4. If you (**continue**) _____ to spy on her, she (**find out**) _____. Then you might never get a date with her.

5. Take a deep breath and just introduce yourself. The world (**not end**) _____ if she (**not be**) _____ interested in you. There are "other fish in the sea."

Caller 3: Hello, this is Antonio. I've known this woman, I'll call her "Alicia," for a few months. I'm not sure if she likes me or not. Sometimes she seems interested, and sometimes she acts like she doesn't care about me. How in the world do you handle someone who's playing hard to get?

6. The next time you talk to "Alicia," try observing her body language. If you (**observe**) _____ carefully, you (**see**) _____ how she reacts to you.

7. For example, if she (**laugh**) _____ at your jokes and (**make**) _____ a lot of eye contact, she (**probably agree**) _____ to go on a date with you.

8. If she (**avoid**) _____ eye contact, (**check**) _____ her watch often, or (**not show**) _____ much interest in what you're saying, she probably (**not go out**) _____ with you.

BONUS
Give your own advice to Natalie, Philip, and Antonio. Use future conditionals (If . . . , + will . . .)

1. Natalie: _____

2. Philip: _____

3. Antonio: _____

Grammar 2

Past Perfect

Nick and Talia are remembering the time they studied together for their college Shakespeare exam. But their memories don't exactly match. Circle the correct way to express their past actions.

1. **Nick:** I was just thinking about the time we studied for our Shakespeare exam. I **had just come/ just came** from soccer practice.

   Talia: Really? I thought that soccer season **was/had been** over in June.

2. **Nick:** It **had started/was starting** to rain and my hair was completely wet and messy. I was a little embarrassed to meet you looking like that.

   Talia: Raining? I don't think so. It **had been/had to be** sunny all week. I remember it clearly. It **was always/had always been** sunny that time of year.

3. **Talia:** **Were we getting/Had we gotten** lunch before we started studying?

   Nick: Before? No. We studied for a while, and then we **went/had gone** to lunch around noon.

4. **Talia:** Oh. Anyway, **didn't we have/hadn't we had** a great time eating at the library café?

   Nick: Yeah, we did! We made jokes about our professors. I **said/have said** that I **always want/ had always wanted** to bring a pillow and an alarm clock to Dr. Custer's class . . .

   Talia: Wait a minute! I **think/had thought** I was the one who said that!

5. **Nick:** Well, the only thing I remember for sure is that after I . . . or you . . . said it, I **turned/had turned** around and . . .

   Talia: We **saw/had seen** Professor Stevens sitting right behind us at the café!

6. **Talia:** How could I forget that? . . . Wow! Well, that was a busy day. I **have never studied/had never studied** so hard in my life until that day! I don't think we even took a break.

   Nick: I'm pretty sure we took a break. We **had had/had** coffee on the library veranda, didn't we?

7. **Talia:** It was a long time ago; I think **we've forgotten/we'd forgotten** a lot, but I **haven't forgotten/hadn't forgotten** how I felt about you . . .

Infinitives after Adjectives and Nouns

A. *Fill in the first blank in each sentence with the correct adjective. You won't use all the adjectives in the box. Then put the verb in parentheses in the correct form. Add* for + *an object pronoun where possible. (Note: The* for *phrase isn't necessary, but it emphasizes the subject of the infinitive.)*

anxious	difficult	easy	embarrassed	ready
lucky	pleased	right	wrong	

1. **Talia:** I'm ___embarrassed___ **(admit)** ___to admit___ that during this investigation I doubted both myself and Nick. But I never gave up hope that he was innocent.

2. **Coach Haskins:** It's _____ **(believe)** _____ Dean would do something like this. I've never had legal problems with any of my players before.

3. **Nick:** I'm _____ **(have)** _____ a second chance with you. I made a big mistake not asking you out back in college.

4. **Talia:** It would be _____ **(regret)** _____ the past. Aren't you _____ **(move)** _____ forward now?

5. **Amy:** I'm so _____ **(find out)** _____ how this whole investigation turns out. I can't wait!

B. *Fill in the first blank in each sentence with the correct noun. You won't use all the nouns in the box. Then put the verb in parentheses in the correct form.*

permission	time	money	potential	person
ability	courage	decision	thing	

1. **Amy:** Nick and Talia will have plenty of ___time___ **(get)** ___to get___ to know each other once they've proven Dean's involvement in this scandal.

2. **Nick:** Oh! I'm so embarrassed. I don't have enough _____ **(leave)** _____ a 20 percent tip.

3. **Talia:** Don't worry; I've got the tip, Nick. Tony gave me _____ **(use)** _____ the *Newsline* expense account.

4. **Tony:** Talia, to be perfectly honest, I wasn't sure you had the _____ **(pull)** _____ this investigation off. Now I realize you're the 1 researcher at *Newsline* who has the _____ **(become)** _____ a really good reporter.

C. Use the adjectives and nouns from the boxes in Exercises A and B to write sentences about yourself.

EXAMPLE: It's not possible for me to play a lot of sports because I don't have much time to spend on activities right now.

1. _____

   _____

2. _____

   _____

Study Tip
Review the Language Functions charts on pages 121–128. Write dialogs with the new phrases. Act them out!

Language Functions

See Appendix 3 to review the language function charts.

Talia and an old friend, Anne, are remembering a trip they took together. Answer the questions about their conversation. Rewrite the boldfaced sentences using the cues in parentheses.

1. **Talia:** **Do you remember when we went to France in high school on an exchange program?**

   Anne: Oh, yeah. That was a lot of fun, wasn't it?

   How else could Talia bring up the memory? (**I was just**)

   _____

2. **Talia:** Do you recall the weather we had?

   Anne: **Don't remind me.** It rained every day. And we had to walk to school!

   What else could Anne say? (**nightmare**)

   _____

3. **Talia:** I remember that you met a nice French guy.

   Anne: I remember that. How could I forget?

   Talia: What was his name?

   Anne: Jean-Michel. **I wish I had stayed in touch with him.**

   What else could Anne say? (**should have**)

   _____

4. **Anne:** Remember how long the flight was?

   Talia: **Sure, I remember.** You slept the whole time, but I couldn't sleep.

   What else could Talia say? (**how could**)

   _____

Application Activities

1. **Writing.** In the story, Nick says he regretted that he didn't ask Talia out for a date when they were in college. Write about something important you wanted to do but decided not to do. Why did you want to do it? Why did you decide not to do it? Was it a good decision? Or do you regret not doing it?

2. **Vocabulary.** Think about vocabulary to describe relationships between people. Write sentences about a couple/couples you know *or* research celebrity gossip pages and write about celebrity couples. Use expressions from this unit and other new expressions to tell about the couple's relationship.

3. **Speaking.** Talk to people about their memories. Use expressions for asking about memories and recalling events. For example, talk to a couple who have been together a long time. Ask them to tell you about how they met, how they decided to stay together, and so on. Are their memories of the events the same or different?

4. **Project.** Research different kinds of advice on dating. Use newspaper or magazine advice columns or advice services on the radio, TV, or Internet. Report some things you learned. Possible topics include finding someone special, breaking up, knowing if someone likes you, and office romances. Use the things you learned to put on a dating advice show in front of the class. "Callers" can ask a panel of experts for their advice. Use future conditionals in your comments to the callers.

Grammar Explanations

This section contains the same grammar explanations that are found on the CD-ROM. They are included here for your quick reference. To view the animated presentation, go to the Grammar section of Unit B.3 in the CD-ROM course.

Grammar 1: Future Conditional

1. We use the **future conditional** to talk about results that will happen under certain conditions. The *if*-clause (the clause beginning with *if*) states the condition. The result clause (the clause that does not begin with *if*) states the result.
   If Nick asks Talia out, she'll say yes.

2. The verb in the ***if*-clause** is in the **present**—even though we are talking about the future.
   The verb in the **result clause** is in the **future** with *will* or *be going to*.
   Talia: If we **leave** now, we**'ll catch** Tony.
   If we **don't leave** now, we**'re going to miss** Tony.

3. You can also use a **modal**, such as *might* and *can*, in the result clause.
   Talia: If we leave now, we **might** see Amy.
   If we see Amy, we **can** tell her what happened.

4. The *if*-clause can come at the beginning or the end of the sentence. The meaning is the same. When the *if*-clause comes first, we put a **comma** after it. When the main clause comes first, we do not use a comma between the 2 clauses.
   Talia: **If we go now,** Tony will still be at the office.
   Tony will still be at the office **if we go now.**

Grammar 2: Past Perfect

1. We use the **past perfect** to talk about something that happened before a specific time in the past.
   It was 8:30. Jackie and Dean **had left** Valentino's.
   This means that Jackie and Dean left before 8:30.

2. We form the **past perfect** with *had* + the past participle. We often use the contraction *'d* with pronoun subjects.
   Nick and Talia already knew each other. They**'d taken** classes together in college.

3. We often introduce the specific time with *by*.
   Talia: My boyfriend and I **had split up** by the middle of the semester.
   In the example, the specific time was the middle of the semester. Talia broke up with her boyfriend before then.

4. We also use the past perfect to show a relationship between 2 past events. We use the **past perfect** for the earlier event and the **simple past** for the later event.
   Dean and Jackie **had left** the restaurant by the time Nick and Talia **ordered** dessert.
   This means that first Dean and Jackie left. Then Nick and Talia ordered dessert.

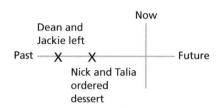

5. We often use *already*, *yet*, and *never* with the past perfect. These words **emphasize** that the event in the past perfect occurred first.
   By the time Talia **studied** for the exam with Nick, she **had already broken up** with her boyfriend.

6. We can use the **simple past** for 2 past events when it is clear which came first. This is often the case when you use *after, before,* or *as soon as* to connect the events.
   Nick **had decided** not to ask Talia out **as soon as** he **heard** that she had a boyfriend.
   Nick **decided** not to ask Talia out **as soon as** he **heard** that she had a boyfriend.
   Both sentences mean that Nick decided not to ask Talia out when he heard that she had a boyfriend.

Grammar 3: Infinitives after Adjectives and Nouns

1. As you know, we can use the infinitive after certain verbs. But we can also use the infinitive after certain adjectives.
   Talia: Are you **ready to go**?
   Many of these adjectives describe a feeling about the action in the infinitive.
   Talia was **anxious to work** on the story.

Other Adjectives That Can Be Followed by the Infinitive	
embarrassed	surprised
happy	pleased
lucky	sorry

2. We can also use the infinitive after some nouns. The noun + infinitive combination often expresses necessity or advice.

> **Nick:** I have a **confession to make**.
>
> Why don't we just take a little **time to enjoy** ourselves?

Here are some more examples:

Do you have **permission to go**?
She's the **person to ask**.
I have a **test to study** for.
It's **time to leave**.

3. We also use **infinitives** after **adjective + noun** combinations.

> **Nick:** That's an **easy mistake to make**.
>
> **Talia:** Jackie really wants to be famous.
>
> **Nick:** But it's a **high price to pay** for fame.

4. We often use *for + a noun or pronoun* before the infinitive when we include the subject of the infinitive.

> **Nick:** It's **important for the federation to hear** the tape.
>
> **Talia:** It's **time for us to go**.

B.4 A Lesson Learned

Listening

🎧 **A. Listen to Track 20.** *Talia, Amy, and Tony are talking about the tape. Each numbered item contains a mistake. Correct the mistakes.*

Talia: I'm too late, right? (1) ~~You aired already~~ the story
You already aired

about Nick on the evening news?

Tony: No, I decided not to. (2) When I haven't heard from you, I decided to wait. . . . (3) As a matter of fact, I am just going to call you.

Talia: It was perfect. I got it all on tape. (4) Jackie said that she poses as a Kicks executive . . .

Amy: No!

Talia: Yes! (5) And they both admitted that there is no Kicks!

Amy: Get out of here!

Talia: (6) And Dean actually had said that he had sent the tape to us . . .

Amy: Unbelievable!

Talia: What's going on? Is this tape player working?

Tony: It's been working just fine. (7) In fact, I just cleaned it last week.

Amy: Try another tape and see if that works.

Tony: Thanks, Amy. (8) I'm just about to try that.

Amy: Did you check that the recording light was on?

Talia: (9) I was checking it after I sat down but too much was going on.

B. Listen to Track 21. *You will hear 3 short news stories. Place the phrases under the correct story.*

all of whom attended	is reported to be doing well
left a track of	one of the original members of
reported to be in stable condition	were hit by
from his previous	were injured

Tornado Devastates County

_____

_____

_____

Baby and Dad Doing Well after Liver Surgery

_____

_____

_____

Rock Star Weds in Ireland

_____

_____

_____

Vocabulary

See Appendix 2 to review the vocabulary terms.

Match the situation in the left column with the action or idea in the right column.

Situation

_d_ 1. There was a lot of tension between Tony and John.

____ 2. Andy and his wife needed to borrow money to buy a house.

____ 3. Amy wanted to borrow Phil's car.

____ 4. Tony and Elisa finished dinner.

____ 5. Amy wanted to put some papers on Talia's desk.

____ 6. Talia was really worried about the deadline for her story.

____ 7. Amy wanted to say something important to Tony.

____ 8. Talia was convinced that Nick was innocent.

____ 9. Ms. Boyd felt that her life was a mess.

____ 10. Talia needed special permission to enter the government office.

Action or Idea

a. She had to clear it with him first.

b. She really wanted to clear his name.

c. They wanted to clear the table before having dessert.

d. They had a discussion to clear the air.

e. She took a walk to clear her head.

f. She had to clear a space first.

g. They had to clear their old debts first.

h. Her *Newsline* press pass cleared the way.

i. She cleared her throat first.

j. She wanted to clear the decks and start over.

Grammar 1

Future in the Past

A. *Talia's plans for tonight keep changing. Read her phone conversations from this evening and fill in each blank with the correct form of the verb in parentheses. Use* am / is / are going to *or* was / were going to.

1. **Mandy:** Hi, Talia. What **(do)** ___are you going to do___ tonight?

   Talia: Well, I **(stay)** _____ home tonight. But what did you have in mind?

   Mandy: How about going out for dinner with the girls around 7:00?

2. **Mandy:** I'm just calling to let you know we **(cancel)** _____ the "girls' night out."

   Talia: Why?

   Mandy: Well, we **(go)** _____ to Club Brasil, but it's closed for repairs. But I **(reschedule)** _____ our get-together for next week, OK?

3. **Josh:** Hi, Talia. Amy and I are watching a movie tonight at her place. Do you want to join us?

   Talia: Some friends and I **(go out)** _____ tonight, but those plans were canceled, so actually I'm free tonight.

B. *Write 2 sentences about things you were going to do this week but didn't do.*

EXAMPLE: ___On Tuesday, I was going to work out at the gym, but I watched a movie instead.___

1. _____

   _____

2. _____

   _____

Passive Causative

A. *Talia and Alex are talking about different machines in their office.*
Fill in the blanks with a causative, have *or* get. *In many cases, either is acceptable. Put the verb in parentheses in its passive form.*

1. **Talia:** Is this video player working all right?

   Alex: Yes, I just **(check)** _____had it checked_____ last week.

2. **Alex:** Don't take that tape player.

   Talia: Why not?

   Alex: I have to **(repair)** _____. Something's wrong with it.

3. **Talia:** Can you fix this DV camera?

   Alex: I can't do it myself. I have to **(service)** _____

   by the manufacturer.

4. **Alex:** Talia, do you know what's wrong with the copy machine? Maybe it's

   out of toner?

   Talia: I don't think so. We just **(replace)** _____ last week.

5. **Talia:** Do you know where the mini-TV is?

   Alex: Oh, that's in the service center. We're **(service)** _____

   right now.

6. **Talia:** What happened to the sound on this videotape?

   Alex: I'm not sure. John is trying to **(restore)** _____

   in the sound lab.

B. *Tell some things you had done or are going to have done. Use* get / have *and different verb tenses.*

   EXAMPLE: ___I've had my ears pierced twice. I'm thinking about having my hair cut tomorrow.___

   1. _____

   2. _____

   3. _____

Grammar 3

Reported Statements

A. *A reporter is doing a special report on a big earthquake that hit the area yesterday at 5:15 p.m. Report the statements using the verb in parentheses. Make the necessary changes in verb tense, pronouns, and time expressions.*

What were you doing right before the earthquake?

1. **Mr. Field:** I was in the teacher's room. I was getting ready to go home.

    (say) __Mr. Field said he had been getting ready to go home.__

2. **Cindy Nakano:** The Drama Club meeting had just ended. I was waiting outside for my mom to pick me up.

    (tell) __Cindy Nakano told me__

    (add) __She added that__

When did you know it was an earthquake?

3. **Mr. Field:** I saw the lockers in the hallway shaking.

    (tell) _____

4. **Cindy Nakano:** All the cars in the street stopped.

    (note) _____

What did you do when you realized it was an earthquake?

5. **Mr. Field:** I got down on the floor, under my desk.

    (state) _____

6. **Cindy Nakano:** I ran to a nearby building and stood in a doorway.

    (say) _____

Is there anything you have to do because of the earthquake?

7. **Mr. Field:** Tomorrow I'm going to have to clean up the mess in the office.

    (complain) _____

8. **Cindy Nakano:** I don't know. The school is probably going to cancel classes this week.

    (say, guess) _____

B. *Think of 2 things you heard people say today and report them. You can use different verbs for reporting (mention, complain, etc.)*

EXAMPLE: __My neighbor mentioned that she was going out of town next week.__

1. _____

2. _____

See Appendix 3 to review the language function charts.

Complete the conversations using appropriate phrases. Use the cues in parentheses.

Jackie and a classmate, Tina, are doing an assignment for class using a video camera.

Jackie: (1) Something _____ (*identifying a problem*) camera. It won't record

properly.

Tina: Did you turn it on and put the tape in correctly?

Jackie: Yes, I did that already. I'm sure I did.

Tina: (2) What we _____ (*suggesting a course of action*) plug it in. The battery

might be dead.

Jackie: Good idea. (3) Let's give _____ (*committing to a course of action*).

Amy and Chris are trying to print a paper they wrote together.

Chris: The printer is acting up again. This is driving me crazy!

Amy: (4) What _____ (*emotional response*). This paper is due in 1 hour!

(5) Have _____ checking _____ (*suggesting a course of action*) the print cartridge?

Chris: I did that already. It still doesn't work.

Amy: I have an idea. (6) Why _____ use a different printer? We can go to

the computer lab and print the paper there.

Chris: OK. Let's do that.

Application Activities

1. **Listening and Grammar.** Listen to a news broadcast or a news interview. Take notes. Afterward, write the main points of the broadcast or interview in reported speech. Pay attention to the verb tenses.

2. **Writing.** Because the conversation in the restaurant wasn't recorded, Talia said that the situation was a "disaster." Have you ever had a similar disaster? Tell what happened. What did you do to recover?

3. **Speaking.** Ask someone you know to describe a problem he or she had in the past (with work, family, school, etc.). Ask them how they solved the problem. Report the details of your conversation to the class using direct and indirect speech and expressions for troubleshooting.

4. **Project.** Find a story from your culture that is entertaining and educational, similar to the story of "The Lost Horse" in the Reading section of the CD-ROM unit. Take notes. Practice telling the story in less than 2 minutes. Use visual aids if possible. Tell your story to the class and answer their questions.

Grammar Explanations

This section contains the same grammar explanations that are found on the CD-ROM. They are included here for your quick reference. To view the animated presentation, go to the Grammar section of Unit B.4 in the CD-ROM course.

Grammar 1: Future in the Past

1. We use the **future in the past** to talk about future plans that we made in the past.
   > **Tony:** I **was** just **going to call** you.

   This means that Tony had planned to call Talia.

2. Most of the time, we use the future in the past to talk about planned events that **didn't happen**.
   > **Talia:** I **was going to check** after we sat down, but too much was going on.

   In the example, Talia had planned to check that the recording light on her tape player was on, but she didn't do it.

3. We form the **future in the past** with *was* or *were* + *going to* + the base form of the verb.
   > Tony **was going to listen** to the tape.
   > Amy and John **were going to listen**, too.

Future in the Past
I **was(n't) going to call** them.
You **were(n't) going to call** them.
He/She/It **was(n't) going to call** them.
We **were(n't) going to call** them.
They **were(n't) going to call** them.

Grammar 2: Passive Causative

1. We use the **passive causative** to talk about services that another person does for us.
   > **Tony:** I **had the tape player cleaned** last week.

   This means that someone cleaned the tape player for Tony. He didn't clean it himself.

2. We can also use the **passive causative** to talk about something that causes something else to happen. We usually use *get* (not *have*) for this meaning.
   > **Talia:** This is the recording that **will get Nick reinstated**.

   This means that Nick will be reinstated because of the recording.

3. We form the **passive causative** with *have* or *get* + a direct object + the past participle of the verb.
   > Talia **gets her hair done** at Fausto's Hair Salon.
   > Talia **has her hair done** at Fausto's Hair Salon.

   These 2 sentences have the same meaning.

4. We use the **passive causative** with all tenses and with modals.
   > John **has his car inspected** every year. (simple present)
   > He **has gotten it done** at the same place since he bought it. (present perfect)
   > He **had it inspected** last week. (simple past)
   > He**'s going to get it painted** next week. (future)
   > He **might have the tires replaced** also. (modal)

5. We use *by* when we mention the person doing the service. We mention the person doing the service only when it provides important information.
   > Amy **is getting her hair cut by** the best hairdresser in town.

   We do **NOT** say: ~~Amy is getting her hair cut by a hairdresser.~~

Grammar 3: Reported Statements

1. A **direct statement** uses the person's **exact words**.

   When we write, we put **quotation marks** around direct statements.
   > Jackie said, "I posed as a Kicks executive."

2. We can also report statements without using the person's exact words. In this case, we use **reported statements**. We often use the word *that* to introduce a reported statement.
   > **Talia** (*to Tony later that evening*): Jackie said **that she had posed as a Kicks executive**.

   You can also leave out the word *that*. The meaning is the same.
   > **Talia:** Jackie said **she had posed as a Kicks executive**.

   We don't use quotation marks in reported statements.

   We do **NOT** write: ~~Jackie said that "she had posed as a Kicks executive."~~

3. The most common **reporting verbs** are *say* and *tell*.
   We use *say* when we don't mention the listener.
   > **Jackie:** Dean, I'm worried.
   > Jackie **said that she was worried**.

   We do **NOT** say: ~~Jackie told that she was worried.~~

   We use *tell* when we mention the listener.
   > Jackie **told Dean that she was worried**.

   We do **NOT** say: ~~Jackie said Dean that she was worried.~~

4. When we report someone's statements, we often change the verb tense. **Simple present** changes to **simple past**.
   > **Dean:** There **is** no Byron Walters.
   > Dean said that there **was** no Byron Walters.

Present continuous changes to **past continuous**.
> **Talia:** I**'m not seeing** anyone.
> Talia said that she **wasn't seeing** anyone.

Simple past changes to **past perfect**.
> **Dean:** I **sent** the phony tape to *Newsline*.
> **Talia:** Dean actually said that he **had sent** the phony tape to us.

Present perfect changes to **past perfect**.
> **Tony:** You**'ve just learned** a lesson the hard way.
> **Amy:** Tony said that she**'d just learned** a lesson the hard way.

5. When the **reporting verb** is in the present, we don't change the verb tense in the reported statement.
> **Talia:** I**'m** really worried about Nick.
> **Amy:** Talia says that she**'s** really worried about Nick.

6. In reported statements, we also make other changes to keep the original meaning.

We change **pronouns** and **possessive adjectives**.
> **Tony:** I**'m** looking for **my** tape player.
> **Talia:** Tony said that **he** was looking for **his** tape player.

We also change time words.
> **Talia:** I met Jackie **yesterday**.
> **Tony** (*the next day*)**:** Talia said that she'd met Jackie **the day before**.

Common Changes in Reported Statements	
Direct Statement	**Reported Statement**
simple present	simple past
present continuous	past continuous
simple past	past perfect
present perfect	past perfect
today	*yesterday*
yesterday	*the day before*
tomorrow	*the next day*
this week	*that week*
last week	*the week before*
next week	*the following week*

C.1 A Canceled Celebration

Listening

🎧 *A. Listen to Track 22. Talia is talking to Nick in her apartment. Correct the phrases in bold in their conversation.*

1. **Talia:** I feel awful. **If I was more careful, we would have the evidence!**

   If I had been more careful, we would have had the evidence.

2. **Nick:** Wow! And **we are supposed to celebrate** tonight.

   _____

3. **Talia:** How stupid! I can't believe I didn't press the right buttons! **I just wish I was more careful.**

   _____

4. **Nick:** And **I hope you'll stop** kicking yourself.

   _____

5. **Talia:** Well, **I'm a professional**! And I want to be a reporter!

   _____

6. **Talia:** I wish **we could go back** and **do it again**.

   _____

7. **Nick:** Well, you can't. Take it from me. I'm an athlete. I know. **You just need to forget the past and move on.**

   _____

8. **Talia:** You're right. What's done is done. Or in this case, what's not done is done.

   Nick: Look, Talia, **if you didn't do such a good job of covering the story, we never would know the truth.**

   _____

   Talia: How can you stay so positive?

🎧 **B. Listen to Track 23.** *Match the beginnings and endings of the sentences.*

_____ **1.** I enjoy life. I am a spontaneous person and I like to

_____ **2.** I feel that my personal life and my professional life are

_____ **3.** I want to contribute

_____ **4.** When people around me are feeling down, I usually try

_____ **5.** I enjoy giving compliments and telling people

_____ **6.** I don't let difficulties and unfortunate events

_____ **7.** I worry a lot that people I am close to will leave me, even though

_____ **8.** If my boss phones me and says that she wants to talk to me in person,

_____ **9.** When I wake up in the middle of the night with a stomachache,

_____ **10.** When I see a glass filled halfway,

a. something to the world.

b. stop me from reaching my goals.

c. act according to how I feel.

d. there is usually no reason to believe that.

e. I usually think it's (half full / half empty).

f. to get them to cheer up and look at the bright side of things.

g. improving all the time.

h. how important they are to me.

i. I usually think it'll pass.

j. I assume it's some bad news.

Study Tip
Watch the characters' expressions and gestures in the video. Repeat what they say and try to imitate their expressions.

BONUS

1. Which of the statements in Exercise B indicate an optimist?

_____

2. Which of the statements indicate a pessimist?

_____

See Appendix 2 to review the vocabulary terms.

Replace the word or phrase in bold with a word or phrase using over.

At the *Newsline* office

1. Tony **supervises** the *Newsline* journalists. His job is to make sure that everyone follows professional standards.

2. Claire is a great proofreader, but yesterday she **missed** a few spelling mistakes in a big news article.

3. John **listened in on** Tony and Talia's conversation about the tape recording. He was really surprised to learn about Talia's mistake.

At the movie theater

4. **Movie theatre clerk:** Here you are—a small popcorn and a soda. That's $12.

    Amy: Twelve dollars? Wait a minute! Aren't you **charging me too much**?

5. **Movie theater clerk:** That's the price, lady. Look, if you can't afford it, don't buy it!

    Amy: Wait, wait, wait. Please don't **make such a big deal out of it**! I'm just asking if that's the right price.

6. **Amy:** Do you want some of this popcorn?

    Talia: Sure . . . thanks. Wow, that's salty! I think you **put too much salt on it**.

At the national team office

7. **Dean:** How many pizzas did you order for the team party?

    Coach: I ordered 25 pizzas, but there are only 15 people here. I think I **guessed wrong about** how many people were coming.

8. **Dean:** I don't know, Coach. I'm pretty hungry. Maybe I can eat them all by myself.

    Coach: No way, Dean. I don't want you to **eat too much**. We need to have you fresh for the match tomorrow.

Wish

A. *Amy has introduced her friend Josh to her friend Mandy. She set up a blind date for them. Josh and Mandy are now on the date and things are* not *going well. Read Mandy's and Josh's thoughts. Change their statements into wishes.*

Josh

1. I brought her yellow roses. Mandy told me that yellow roses mean "friendship" and red roses mean "romance." I didn't know that.

   I wish I hadn't brought her yellow roses.

   _____

2. I didn't compliment Mandy on her outfit. How stupid of me!

   _____

   _____

3. I said, "You remind me of my mother." I shouldn't have said that. Dumb, dumb, dumb!

   _____

4. The taxi driver won't drive faster. We'll never get to the play on time. Come on, hurry up!

   _____

Mandy

5. Josh brought me flowers. I'm allergic to flowers.

   _____

6. Josh doesn't like my outfit. He didn't say anything about it.

   _____

7. I sound nervous. Why can't I calm down?

   _____

8. The taxi driver is driving so fast. It's dangerous.

   _____

BONUS
Write another one of Josh's wishes or Mandy's wishes.

_____

B. *Make wishes for yourself. Use the words provided in parentheses.*

EXAMPLE: **(wouldn't)** <u>I wish my friend Alex wouldn't call me so late at night.</u>

1. Something you don't want someone (friend, roommate, classmate, co-worker, relative, neighbor, pet, etc.) to do

   (wouldn't) _____

2. Something you want someone to do

   (would) _____

3. Something you would like to be able to do

   (could) _____

4. A quality about yourself (your personality) that you would like to change

   (were / weren't + adjective) _____

5. Something you did / didn't do that you regret

   (had / hadn't + past participle) _____

Grammar 2

Past Unreal Conditional

A. *After their blind date, both Josh and Mandy had some regrets. They both called Amy to tell her what happened. Change their statements in bold into sentences with past conditionals (would have, wouldn't have, might have, might not have).*

1. **Josh: She probably looked disappointed because I gave her yellow roses instead of red.** I blew it!

   <u>If I had given her red roses instead of yellow roses, she</u>

   <u>wouldn't have looked so disappointed.</u>

   Amy: Now don't overreact, Josh. Mandy didn't appreciate the yellow roses because she is allergic to flowers.

2. **Josh: I felt sick after dinner. I just ate too much because I didn't know what to talk about.** What an idiot I am!

   <u>If I</u> _____, <u>I wouldn't</u> _____

   Amy: Oh, Josh. You always overeat when you're nervous.

3. **Mandy: Josh felt sick after dinner because I made him uncomfortable.** It's all my fault!

   _____, _____ felt sick.

   Amy: No, it had nothing to do with you, Mandy. He was sick because he ate too much at Valentino's. Josh always overeats when he's nervous.

4. Mandy: Josh didn't compliment me because I didn't wear my best black dress. I'm so stupid!

_____, _____ complimented me.

    Amy: No, Mandy! I'm sure you looked great. Josh didn't compliment you on your outfit because he was really nervous.

B. *Think of a past situation you regret. Write 2 sentences about it using past conditionals.*

    EXAMPLE: I didn't go to my high school reunion. If I hadn't been so busy, I would have gone. If I'd gone,

       I would have seen many of my old friends again.

_____

_____

Grammar 3

Be supposed to

Fill in the blanks with the verb provided in parentheses and a form of be supposed to.

1. Jackie: When I was a teenager, I planned out my acting career. I **(get)** _____ a part in a movie by the time I was 19. I'm 24 now, but I'm still trying.

    Richard: Well, you have to have patience. Good things come to those who wait!

2. Amy: It's 10:00 a.m. I **(finish)** _____ scanning these documents by 5:00 p.m. Oh, well, I have plenty of time. I'll do them after lunch.

    Ms. Boyd: I don't know, Amy. There's no time like the present!

3. Josh: This DVD player isn't working very well. It **(not open)** _____ when it's playing.

    Amy: Well, Josh, you only paid $19 for it—you get what you pay for!

4. Dean: My mother taught me that a Bishop **(not be)** _____ satisfied with less than the best. So I'm going to be the best player in the league—I know I will!

    Jackie: That's right, Dean. The sky's the limit!

5. Tony: As professional journalists, we **(look)** _____ at the facts. Looking at the facts, I really thought Nick was going to be guilty.

    John: Well, you know, Tony, looks can be deceiving!

6. Claire: I have to choose between dating Will and dating Paul. How **(make)** _____ I _____ such a difficult decision?

    Ms. Boyd: Well, Claire, you know what they say: Follow your heart!

Language Functions

See Appendix 3 to review the language function charts.

Fill in the conversations with phrases from the boxes.

Claire is talking to her friend Andres about his job at the café.

be so hard on yourself	don't worry about it	feel bad
have let that happen	I blew it	

Andres: I got fired from my job at the café. I'm really upset about it.

Claire: I'm sorry to hear that.

Andres: No, (1)_____. I was late for work 3 times last week.

Claire: Oh, I see. Well, (2)_____. You'll find another job.

Andres: I shouldn't (3)_____.

Claire: Don't (4)_____. What's done is done.

Andres: I know. But I still (5)_____.

Amy and Jin are talking about their group assignment.

How could she do that	my fault	made a terrible mistake
nothing we can do about it now	worry about it	

Amy: Oh, no! Deborah forgot to bring the PowerPoint presentation.

Jin: What? (6)_____?

Amy: Well, it's all (7)_____. I was supposed to call her to remind her, and I forgot to call her. I'm sorry, I (8)_____.

Jin: Well, don't (9)_____. There's (10)_____. We'll just have to do it next week.

Application Activities

1. **Grammar.** Write 3 to 4 sentences about your wishes. Choose 1 of the following:

   • If you could wish for 3 things, what would they be? Be specific about what you would choose and why. Use present wishes.
   • Write about something that happened in the past that you wish you could change. Use past wishes and past conditionals.

2. **Vocabulary.** Use your dictionary. Find 3 verbs that start with *over-*. Now find 3 more verbs with the prefix *under-*. *Under* often has the meaning *small* or *too little* (for example, *under*charge, *under*age), but not always (for example, *understand, undergo*). Does the prefix *under-* in your new words have this meaning?

3. **Writing.** Pessimists and optimists can both offer something to a group. Imagine you are working on a project for school or work with both a pessimist and an optimist. What might the pessimist contribute to the project? What might the optimist contribute? Who would you rather work with and why? Which style is closest to your own?

4. **Speaking.** In the story, Nick tells Talia something his grandmother always used to say: "The truth will win out." What did you learn from a grandparent or a parent? Share the knowledge with your classmates.

5. **Project.** The Task Listening in this unit has an "Optimist Test." Give this test to several people: Read them the questions and record their responses, plus any additional comments they have. You can add other questions to the test if you wish. Compile the results of your tests. Give a presentation to the class. Are most people optimistic or pessimistic? Give examples.

Grammar Explanations

This section contains the same grammar explanations that are found on the CD-ROM. They are included here for your quick reference. To view the animated presentation, go to the Grammar section of Unit C.1 in the CD-ROM course.

Grammar 1: *Wish*

1. We use *wish* + the **simple past** to make a wish about something in the **present**.
   Talia: I **wish** I **had** a recording of their conversation.

   This means that Talia doesn't have a recording now, but she wants one.

   Amy: I **wish** Talia **didn't work** all the time.

   In the example, Talia works all the time, but Amy doesn't want her to.

   When the verb is *be*, we usually use *were* after *wish*, even for singular subjects.
   Talia: I **wish** I **were** that optimistic.

2. We use *wish* + the **past perfect** to talk about things **in the past** that we **regret**.
   Talia: I just **wish** I **had been** more careful.

   In the example, Talia wasn't careful, and she regrets it.

3. We use *wish* + *would* + the **base form of the verb** to express a wish for someone to act in a different way.
   Nick: And I **wish** you **would** stop kicking yourself.

   We don't use *will* after *wish*.

   We do **NOT** say: ~~I wish you will stop kicking yourself.~~

4. We use *wish* + *could* to express a wish about an **ability in the present**.
   Talia: I **wish** I **could** go back and do it over.

   We don't use *can* after *wish*.

   We do **NOT** say: ~~I wish I can go back and do it over.~~

Grammar 2: Past Unreal Conditional

1. We use the **past unreal conditional** to talk about past conditions and results that never happened. The *if*-clause expresses the unreal condition. The result clause expresses the unreal result.
   Talia: **If I had been more careful, we would have had the evidence!**

   This means that Talia wasn't careful and as a result they don't have the evidence.

   We often use the past unreal conditional to express **regrets** about what happened in the past.
   Talia: **If I hadn't messed it up, we'd have the tape now.**

   In the example, Talia regrets that she messed up the recording.

2. The verb in the *if*-clause is in the **past perfect**.
   Nick: If you **hadn't done** such a good job, we'd never have known the truth.

We form the verb in the **result clause** with *would have* + **the past participle**.
   Nick: If you **hadn't done** such a good job, we'd never **have known** the truth.

Notice that in conversation, we often use the contraction *'d* for *would* and *wouldn't* for *would not*. We also use the contraction *'d* for *had* and *hadn't* for *had not*.

3. We can also use the **modals** *could, should,* or *might* in the result clause.
   If Talia **had had** more time, she **might have remembered** to check the buttons.
   If she **had checked** the buttons, she **could've prevented** her mistake.

   We often use the contractions *could've, should've,* or *might've* in conversation.

4. The *if*-clause can come at the beginning or the end of the sentence. The meaning is the same. Notice that in writing, we use a **comma** after the *if*-clause when it comes first.
   Talia: **If I had been more careful,** we would've had the evidence!
   We would've had the evidence **if I had been more careful.**

Grammar 3: *Be supposed to*

1. We use the expression *be supposed to* to express **expectations**—feelings or beliefs about how something should be or how someone should behave.
   Talia: I'm **supposed to** be a professional!

   Talia means that people expect her to act in a professional way.

   Liza: The movie **is supposed to** start at 5:05.

   This means that according to a schedule, the movie should start at 5:05.

   John: Valentino's **is supposed to** be a great restaurant.

   This means that people say Valentino's is great.

2. We use *be supposed to* in the **simple present** to express **present** or **future expectations**.
   John **is supposed to** be in the office **now**.
   He **isn't supposed to** be in the office **tomorrow**.

3. We use *be supposed to* in the **simple past** to express **past expectations**.

> Nick **was supposed to** arrive at 7:00.
>
> Talia **was supposed to** press both buttons, but she didn't.

> **Nick:** We **were supposed to** be celebrating tonight.

Notice that we often use *was* or *were supposed to* to talk about an event that didn't happen as planned.

4. To express expectations, we use a form of ***be*** + ***supposed to*** + the **base form of the verb**.

> **Talia:** I know we**'re supposed to** be celebrating.

Be supposed to
I **am (not) supposed to be** here.
You **are (not) supposed to be** here.
He/She/It **is (not) supposed to be** here.
We **are (not) supposed to be** here.
They **are (not) supposed to be** here.
I **was (not) supposed to be** here.
You **were (not) supposed to be** here.
He/She/It **was (not) supposed to be** here.
We **were (not) supposed to be** here.
They **were (not) supposed to be** here.

C.2 Jackie's Big Scene

Listening

🎧 **A. Listen to Track 24.** *Jackie stops by Talia's apartment. Complete the conversation.*

Jackie: . . . Oh, hello, Nick. Remember me?

Nick: (1)_____.

Talia: What are you doing here?

Jackie: Do you have a video camera? . . . Do you want a

(2)_____?

One that (3)_____ all really

famous?

Talia: What's the catch?

Jackie: No catch. Just one (4)_____. If Nick agrees

(5)_____ charges against me, (6)_____ the

whole truth.

🎧 **B. Listen to Track 25.** *Talia is interviewing Jackie. Complete the interview.*

Jackie: I knew Nick usually went to the juice bar at the health club, and I met him there.

Talia: And then?

Jackie: Then, posing as this woman from Kicks, I (1)_____ Nick to

come to my office to discuss an endorsement.

Talia: And did he?

Jackie: Well, I (2)_____ an office, you know. So I

(3)_____ him in the Gower Building lobby and

(4)_____ him to lunch. I (5)_____ the whole

conversation. Dean (6)_____ from there. He doctored the tape

to make it sound like Nick had accepted a bribe.

Talia: Why did you decide to tell the truth now?

Jackie: Dean (7)_____ me to some big-shot movie director, and I

believed him. Well, I just (8)_____ that Dean had been lying the

whole time.

🎧 **C. Listen to Track 26.** *Read each statement of advice. If the statement is consistent with (similar to) the speaker's idea, write* **C.** *If the statement is inconsistent with (different from) the speaker's idea, write* **I.**

_____ 1. Try to learn as much as you can about the person you are going to interview.

_____ 2. Take lots of notes about the person's history so that you can memorize the facts.

_____ 3. Talk to the guest for a while before the interview actually begins.

_____ 4. It's important to put the guest at ease during the first part of the interview.

_____ 5. Avoid humor during the interview. It's important to be serious.

_____ 6. Write down 8 or 10 specific questions in advance.

_____ 7. You and the guest should each talk about half of the time.

_____ 8. Be sure to thank the guest and show your appreciation for the interview.

Vocabulary

See Appendix 2 to review the vocabulary terms.

Complete each sentence with the correct phrasal verb in the box. Be careful of the verb tense and form.

come about	come across	come between	come by
come down to	come down with	come forward	come out
come through	come up		

1. Several laptop computers were missing from the health club. They're having trouble finding the thief because no witnesses are willing to _____.

2. When the police investigated, it _____ that someone who works at the health club was stealing the computers.

3. Dean and Brian had always been great teammates, but their opinions about Nick have _____ them. Now they hardly talk to each other.

4. Patty missed a few days of work last week. She _____ a bad cold and had to stay home in bed.

5. Patty has had a hard time recently. She's been sick, and she's had some trouble at school and with her boss at work. But she's an optimist—I'm sure she'll _____ OK!

6. Hey, Nick. Look, here are some old photos of you and me. I _____ them when I was cleaning out my desk.

7. I can't make it to the meeting this afternoon. Please let me know if something important _____.

Grammar 1

Present Unreal Conditional

A. *The* Newsline *office is having a staff meeting. They are discussing new ideas and possible changes in the office. Complete the conditional sentences by writing the correct form of the verbs in parentheses.*

1. **Talia:** If Tony (**promote**) _____promoted_____ me to a reporter, Amy (**take**) _____could take_____ my job as a researcher.

2. **Amy:** The secretary (**help**) _____ the researchers more if he (**have**) _____ so many other projects to work on.

3. **John:** If we (**install**) _____ a screen to separate my desk from Ms. Boyd's, she and I (**have**) _____ more privacy.

4. **Jeremy:** If Café Starr (**prepare**) _____ a special lunch every Friday, the employees (**not need**) _____ to leave the office for lunch on such a busy day. They (**be**) _____ a lot happier, too!

5. **John:** If we (**include**) _____ a special news feature for children, they (**watch**) _____ part of the program with their parents. That (**encourage**) _____ children to become interested in news at an early age.

6. **Amy:** If *Newsline* (**offer**) _____ free membership to a health club, the employees (**exercise**) _____ more. It (**not cost**) _____ too much and the employees (**feel**) _____ better about themselves. And if the employees (**feel**) _____ better, they (**perform**) _____ better at their jobs.

B. *Write two suggestions. Suggest ways to improve your English class, your workplace, your home, and so on. Use present unreal conditionals. Try to add on to your suggestions where possible.*

EXAMPLE: ___If we had more group projects, we might have more fun in English class.___

1. _____

  _____

2. _____

  _____

Past Perfect Continuous

Jackie is daydreaming about being a famous actress. In her imagination, she's giving a television interview about her successful acting career. Circle the correct verb form or verb tense.

1. **Interviewer:** Jackie, when you started filming the new Jamie Blonde movie, *High Spy*, **had you been taking / have you been taking** any karate or martial arts classes?

2. **Jackie:** No. **I hadn't / wasn't**. I just have a natural talent. I **hadn't / hadn't been** dieting or working out either. I've always **been / being** slim and attractive.

3. **Interviewer:** I see. . . . Let's talk about the beginning of your acting career. By 2004, you **had been struggling / were struggling** to become an actress for more than 5 years.

4. **Jackie:** That's true. Up to that time, **I'd been taking / I've been taking** small parts in movies. For example, **I appeared / have appeared** as an "extra" in 1 scene in the fantasy film *Queen of the Jewels*. Perhaps you noticed me?

5. **Interviewer:** Let's talk about the famous role that really started your career: in the Dean Bishop–Nick Crawford scandal a few years ago.

   Jackie: Oh, yes, *that*. I **dreamed / had been dreaming** about becoming an actress for years when my big break finally came.

6. **Jackie:** I **play / played** the part of a VP of marketing. I **had been studying / am studying** improvisation, so I knew how to act without a script.

7. **Interviewer:** **Did Dean come up with / Had Dean been coming up with** the idea to frame Nick?

   Jackie: Yes, **he did / he had**. It was all his idea.

8. **Interviewer:** You felt that Dean treated you unfairly?

   Jackie: Yes, I **had / did**. Dean **has been living / had been living** in my shadow for a long time. He **didn't want / hadn't been wanting** me to succeed as an actress.

9. **Jackie:** When Dean double crossed me, I decided to come forward.

   Interviewer: It was the right thing to do. You **saved / had saved** Nick Crawford!

   Jackie: Yes! It certainly *was* the right thing to do—for Nick and for my acting career. I **am not getting / hadn't been getting** very many parts at all, but when *Newsline* broke the story, I **started receiving / had been starting to receive** hundreds of offers!

Grammar 3

Should have

A. *Complete the sentences with* should have *or* shouldn't have *and the correct form of the verb in parentheses. Be sure to use appropriate pronouns.*

1. **Amy:** Uh-oh! Claire made a big mistake in this report.

   Talia: **(ask)** _She should have asked us_ for help.

2. **Talia:** I had a great time on my date with Nick, but my feet were killing me the whole time!

   Amy: **(wear)** _____ those shoes. The heels are too high.

3. **Josh:** I made you a special dinner.

   Amy: Wow! Thank you! But **(go)** _____ to so much trouble! It must have taken a long time.

4. **Tony:** Ugh! I wish I hadn't gone out in the rain! **(bring)** _____ an umbrella!

   Elisa: Oh, sweetheart, you're all wet! Let me get you a towel.

5. **Tony:** **(report)** _____ that story about the police department without my permission! *Newsline* is in big trouble because of it.

   Jeremy: I'm sorry, Tony. I felt it was the right thing to do.

6. **Josh:** **(order)** _____ the lasagna.

   Amy: Well, it's not too late. Let's call the waiter.

B. *Decide whether the speakers from Exercise A are expressing* advice *about the past* (**A**), blame (**B**), *or* regret (**R**). *Write* **A**, **B**, *or* **R** *on the line.*

  _A_   **1.** Talia   _____   **3.** Amy   _____   **5.** Tony

  _____   **2.** Amy   _____   **4.** Tony   _____   **6.** Josh

C. *Now write 2 short dialogs about situations in your life. Use* should have *or* shouldn't have *to express* advice, blame, *or* regret.

   EXAMPLE: _Your sister: I got your new dress dirty!_____

              _You: You should have been more careful! Now I can't wear it tonight!_____

1. _____

   _____

2. _____

   _____

Language Functions

See Appendix 3 to review the language function charts.

Complete the conversations with an appropriate phrase. Use the cues in parentheses.

Helen and Patty are talking about their plans.

Patty: Hey, what are you doing this weekend?

Helen: I'm going to my high school reunion. (1) (*express enthusiasm*)

_____

Patty: I bet.

Helen: What about you? What are you going to do?

Patty: I have to work this weekend. (2) (*express reluctance*) _____

Helen: (3) (*give a sympathetic response*) _____

Alex and Claire are talking about their plans for a 3-day weekend.

Alex: Hi, Claire. What are your plans for the long weekend?

Claire: I'm going to Florida to visit my mother. She's been sick recently. (4) (*express worry*)

_____

Alex: (5) (*give a sympathetic response*) _____ I know that can be tough.

Claire: Yeah. What about you?

Alex: I'm going to Atlanta. My father is having a retirement party. He's been working at his company for 25 years, and they're going to give him a farewell party. To tell the truth, (6) (*express apathy*) _____

Claire: I know what you mean. But I'm sure he'll be glad you're there!

Application Activities

Study Tip
As you watch the CD-ROM video, list words and phrases that are difficult to pronounce. Repeat these words every day.

1. **Grammar.** State 3 things that would make your life easier. Explain how they would make your life easier. Use present unreal conditionals (*If I had . . . I would . . .*) in your response. Also state 3 things that would improve other peoples' lives or 3 things that would make life on Earth better! For example, *If people understood other cultures, the world would be more peaceful.*

2. **Vocabulary.** *Come* and *go* are 2 very common verbs in English. There are many expressions and idioms with *come* and *go*. Make a list with 2 columns: expressions using *come* and expressions using *go*. Try to come up with at least 10 expressions in each column. You can use your dictionary (such as *Longman Idioms Dictionary* or *Longman Advanced American Dictionary*) or you can ask other English speakers to help you make your list. Come on, have a go!

3. **Writing.** Do you think the use of video cameras in public places is an invasion of privacy? Should it be limited? Express your opinion. Think about situations involving the police, the government, stores, reality TV shows, and so on.

4. **Speaking.** Talk to people about some plans that you have (for example, vacation, school, career, weekend activities, purchases, etc.). Ask them about their plans. Use expressions for expressing enthusiasm, apathy, and so on.

5. **Project.** This unit deals with regrets, things we should have done or shouldn't have done. Find a song in English that deals with regrets, such as Johnny Cash's "Folsom Prison Blues" or Daryl Hall's "Kiss on my List" or Frank Sinatra's "My Way." Bring an original recording of the song to class and teach the class the lyrics to the song. Play the song and discuss these questions with the class: *What is the song about? What does the singer regret?*

Grammar Explanations

This section contains the same grammar explanations that are found on the CD-ROM. They are included here for your quick reference. To view the animated presentation, go to the Grammar section of Unit C.2 in the CD-ROM course.

Grammar 1: Present Unreal Conditional

1. We use the **present unreal conditional** to talk about present conditions and results that are not real. The *if*-clause expresses the unreal condition. The result clause expresses the unreal result.

   > **If Nick had the evidence, he would be very happy.**

   This means that Nick does not have the evidence and, as a result, he isn't very happy.

   > **If Talia didn't work so hard, she would have more time for fun.**

   This means that Talia works hard and, as a result, she doesn't have time for fun.

2. The verb in the ***if*-clause** is in the **simple past**, but its meaning is present.

   > **Talia:** If I **had** his phone number now, I'd call him.

   The verb in the **result clause** is ***would*** + the **base form** of the verb.

   > **Talia:** If I had his phone number now, I**'d call** him.

   Notice that in conversation, we often use the contraction ***'d*** for ***would*** and ***wouldn't*** for ***would not***.

   We don't use *would* in the *if*-clause.

   We do **NOT** say: ~~If I would have his phone number~~ . . .

3. In addition to *would*, we can also use the **modals** *could, should,* or *might* in the result clause.

   > **Talia:** If I told your coach, the Soccer Federation **might** let you play again.

   > **Nick:** If we had the proof, I **could** play again.

4. When the verb in the *if*-clause is a form of *be*, we use ***were*** for all subjects.

   > **Talia:** If **Tony and John were** here, they would help us.

   > If **Amy were** here, she would help us.

5. We often use ***If I were you*** to give advice.
   > **Nick:** **If I were you,** I wouldn't blame myself.

6. The *if*-clause can come at the beginning or the end of the sentence. The meaning is the same. Notice that in writing, we use a **comma** after the *if*-clause when it comes first.

   > **Nick:** **If he believed you,** it wouldn't matter.

   > It wouldn't matter **if he believed you.**

Grammar 2: Past Perfect Continuous

1. We use the **past perfect continuous** to talk about something that was in progress before a specific time in the past. The **past perfect continuous** focuses on the continuation of an action, not the result.

   > **Tony:** Talia arrived at 10:00. **I'd been waiting for 3 hours** to hear the tape.

   This means that Tony began waiting at 7:00—3 hours before Talia arrived.

   Remember, we usually don't use continuous forms with non-action verbs.

   We do **NOT** say: ~~Tony had been knowing Talia for several years.~~

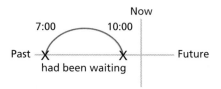

2. We form the past perfect continuous with ***had been*** + the **base form** of the verb + ***-ing***.

   > **Jackie:** I just found out that Dean **had been lying** the whole time.

   Remember, in conversation we often use **contractions** with pronouns.

   We also use the contraction *hadn't* for *had not*.
   > He **hadn't** been practicing with the team.

Past Perfect Continuous

I'd been working all day.
You'd been working all day.
He/She/It'd been working all day.
We'd been working all day.
They'd been working all day.

---

3. We often use ***by*** to introduce the specific time in the past.
   > **Tony:** **By 10:00**, I'd been waiting for 3 hours.

4. We also use the **past perfect continuous** to show a relationship with another past action. The earlier action is in the past perfect continuous. The later action is in the **simple past**.

   > **Jackie:** I just **found out** that Dean **had been lying** the whole time.

   In this example, first Dean lied to Jackie. Then, later, Jackie found out about it.

   > **Amy:** It was late. When Talia finally **arrived**, Tony and I **had been waiting** for 3 hours.

   In this example, first Tony and Amy started waiting, then Talia arrived.

Grammar 3: *Should have*

1. We use ***should have*** + the **past participle** to give advice about something that happened in the past.

   Marta: You **should have worn** a different outfit. Jeans were too informal.

2. We often use *should have* and *should not have* to express **regrets**.

   Jackie: I **should have known** better. I **should not have trusted** Dean.

   We can also use *should have* and *should not have* to express **blame**.

   Jackie: It's your fault. You **should have kept** your promises.

3. In conversation, we often shorten *should* and *have* to ***should've*** and *should not* and *have* to ***shouldn't've***. Do not use these contractions in writing.

   Jackie: I should have known better. I shouldn't have trusted him.

   I **should've** known better. I **shouldn't've** trusted him.

4. We also use ***should have*** to ask questions and give short answers.

   Marta: Should Jackie **have** confessed?
   Bill: Yes, she **should have**.
   Chris: No, she **shouldn't have**.

C.3 Hard Evidence

Listening

🎧 **A. Listen to Track 27.** *Nick is talking with Coach Haskins and Dean. Write the name of the speaker in front of each line:* **Nick, Dean, Coach,** *or* **Jackie.** *Then find the best paraphrase (line with similar meaning in this situation).*

Original line

Nick	1.	You're just the 2 people I wanted to see.
_____	2.	Sorry, man, tough break.
_____	3.	"Don't do the crime if you can't do the time."
_____	4.	That's the smartest thing I've ever heard you say.
_____	5.	I was very convincing, if I must say so myself.
_____	6.	Dean took care of that.
_____	7.	I'd keep quiet if I were you.
_____	8.	My conversation with her was not the only one she recorded.
_____	9.	This is crazy!
_____	10.	I don't know what to say.
_____	11.	Thanks, Coach.
_____	12.	There's someone I have to go talk to.

Paraphrase

6	a.	He's the one who actually did it.
____	b.	I can't really express my feelings about this.
____	c.	I appreciate your sympathy.
____	d.	I can't believe this is happening to me.
____	e.	I'm a great actor, actually.
____	f.	I really want to talk with both of you.
____	g.	You shouldn't talk about it.
____	h.	Other recordings were made also.
____	i.	If you're not willing to take responsibility for the results of your action, don't try it.
____	j.	I have to go see a special person now.
____	k.	You don't realize that you'll have to take your own advice.
____	l.	Too bad!

🎧 **B. Listen to Track 28.** *Nick is in the* Newsline *office talking with Talia, Tony, and Amy. Match each expression to a statement describing the speaker's feeling or reaction.*

_c_   **1.** Depends on what?   **a.** Nick is relieved.

_____ **2.** No problem.   **b.** Amy is happy for Talia.

_____ **3.** This has been a nightmare!   **c.** Tony is wondering what Nick is thinking.

_____ **4.** Just remember . . .   **d.** Tony is reminding Talia of some advice.

_____ **5.** Of course he does!   **e.** Tony is happy to schedule the interview for later.

🎧 **C. Listen to Track 29.** *A man is talking about a dream. Check (✓) 1 phrase in each pair that the man uses.*

1.	✓	recurring nightmare	_____	repeating nightmare
2.	_____	it ended differently	_____	it ended in a different way
3.	_____	I start to feel lost	_____	I start to feel I'm getting lost
4.	_____	out of the corner of my eye	_____	off to the side
5.	_____	heart beating wildly	_____	heart beating fast
6.	_____	narrow, crowded stage	_____	wide, empty stage
7.	_____	waiting for me to speak	_____	waiting for me to perform
8.	_____	blue velvet robe	_____	red velvet cape
9.	_____	this incredible song	_____	this beautiful song
10.	_____	starts shouting	_____	starts applauding
11.	_____	shaking hands with everyone	_____	congratulating everyone
12.	_____	looking into my eyes	_____	looking at my face
13.	_____	hit it on the head	_____	pat it on the head

Vocabulary

See Appendix 2 to review the vocabulary terms.

Talia and her friends are at a family wedding reception, talking about different people. Fill in the missing words in the figurative expressions in the conversation with words from the box.

eye	fit	hot	looks	loud
smooth	soft	thin	tired	warm

1. **Talia:** Look at Andy's suit. Bright red!

    Amy: I've never seen such a _____ color for a suit!

2. **Amy:** Did you notice Olivia's new hair style?

    Talia: Yes, that caught my _____ right away. Very cool.

3. **Josh:** Why is your Uncle Harry so upset?

    Talia: I don't know, but he's always angry. He has such a _____ temper. He's always throwing a _____ about something!

4. **Josh:** Well, Harry's wife is really different. She's so nice.

    Amy: Yes, she is. She gave me such a _____ welcome when I arrived.

5. **Josh:** Is that Amy dancing with your cousin Wally?

    Talia: Yes, he's such a _____ talker. He just asks for something, and everyone immediately says "yes."

6. **Celia:** What do you think of the band?

    Josh: Actually, I don't care for this kind of _____ rock. I like music with a stronger beat!

7. **Amy:** Uh-oh, here comes Wally Stevens. He's been stealing _____ at you all night.

    Wally: Well, hello. You must be one of Talia's friends from work. Would you care to dance?

    Celia: Oh, thank you, but I can't. I have a . . . a sprained . . . wrist . . .

    Amy: A sprained wrist? Celia, that's a pretty _____ excuse!

8. **Josh:** Are those your parents over there, Talia? They're very attractive.

    Amy: Yes, Talia got her good looks from her father. He's a plastic surgeon.

    Talia: Oh, Amy. Very funny! You always tell such _____ jokes!

Grammar 1

Future Continuous

A. *Dean, Jackie, Talia, Nick, and Tony are doing things 1 week from now. All of these activities take place in the near future. Write future statements. Choose between the simple future and future continuous.*

One week from now

1. Dean is sitting at home alone. He's thinking, "Why me?" He is thinking about another scheme to frame Nick.
2. Jackie is doing interviews for 5 national talk shows. Everyone in the country knows who she is.
3. Talia and Amy are sunbathing on a beautiful beach. They are sipping cold lemonade.
4. Talia is thinking about her new position as a reporter at *Newsline*.
5. Tony is reviewing resumes from background researchers who want Talia's old job.
6. Nick is practicing with the soccer team. His teammates are happy for him.
7. Nick is thinking about Talia and wondering if he should call her.
8. Nick is discussing an endorsement deal with Steps, a *real* athletic shoe company.

Statements about actions next week

1. Next week, Dean ___will be sitting at home alone. He will be thinking, "Why me?" He will decide to___ ___plan another scheme to frame Nick.___

2. Next week, Jackie _____

   _____

3. Next week at this time, Talia and Amy _____

   _____

4. One week from now, Talia _____

   _____

5. At this time next week, Tony _____

   _____

6. A week from today, Nick _____

   _____

7. Next week, Nick _____

   _____

8. At this time next week, Nick _____

   _____

B. *Write about some plans or predictions for next week. Use the* future continuous *to talk about things that will be in progress at a specific time in the future.*

EXAMPLE: On Sunday afternoon, I'm going to be playing tennis with my friend Ana.

1. _____

2. _____

3. _____

Grammar 2

Object Adjective Clauses

Talia had an unusual dream a few nights ago. She is telling Amy about the dream. Correct the errors in the object adjective clauses.

1. In my dream, I was on a black sand beach **that I had never been to ~~the beach~~** before.

2. I bent down and picked up some sand. The sand **that I picked it up** turned a silver color.

3. I looked up and a white castle in the distance caught my eye. A man **which I had seen earlier** came to me and told me that the castle was a gift **a kind king had given it to me**. I started walking toward the castle.

4. When I got to the castle, I walked into the garden. Suddenly, a bird grabbed a green apple from a tree and let it fall in front of me. I ate some of the green apple **whom the bird had dropped it**.

5. At this point, I realized that something strange was happening. My beautiful teeth, **I had brushed them so carefully for years**, were falling out! I felt horrible. Then I woke up.

Talia told her dream to Amy. Here is Amy's interpretation. Correct the errors in the object adjective clauses.

6. The black sand beach represents a mystery **that you have been experiencing it**. The silver sand represents a feeling of justice in your life **who you are having right now**.

7. The castle **about that you dreamed** is a reward for your recent success. The white color **that is it painted** represents truth and optimism.

8. The green apple **that was being eaten it** reveals a new love in your life.

9. The teeth **whom you lost** symbolize that you are fearful about something—maybe about your relationship with Nick. But this is a good sign—it is a warning not to be afraid of what happens between you and him.

Passive Modals

Read each conversation. Make a passive sentence using the cues in parentheses.

1. **Roshawn:** Nick, do you want to go out for dinner after practice?

    Nick: Sorry, I can't. **(I / going to / interview / Talia Santos from *Newsline*).**

    I'm going to be interviewed by Talia Santos from Newsline.

2. **Nick:** I'm really glad I'm back on the team again.

    Brian: So are we, Nick. **(We / can't / beat / with you on the team).**

    _____

3. **Amy:** Are you going to record the interview?

    Talia: Of course, I am. **(The interview / has to / record / on video).** This time, I'll be very careful.

    _____

4. **John:** Are we ready to air the Nick Crawford story tonight?

    Tony: Not yet. **(The story / can't / air / without Talia's interview).**

    _____

5. **Talia:** Tony, I can't make it back to the office for the 5 o'clock meeting.

    Tony: That's OK, Talia. **(The meeting / can / reschedule / for tomorrow morning).**

    _____

6. **Talia:** I found out a lot of information about the scandal. Should I tell the police?

    Tony: Not yet. **(Coach Haskins / ought to / tell / first).**

    _____

Language Functions

See Appendix 3 to review the language function charts.

Complete each conversation with the best phrases. Use the phrases in the boxes.

believe that	get so upset	That really burns

Patty: Mark, I have some bad news. I lost that Express Mail envelope you asked me to send.

Mark: What? I can't (1)_____! That was an application to a summer program in Japan!

Patty: I'm sorry. It was a mistake.

Mark: (2)_____ me up.

Patty: Calm down, don't (3)_____. Look, I'll make it up to you. I'll help you fill out another one right now.

How dare he	ticks me off	won't do any good	an outrage

Adam: Professor Smith has decided to give the exam tomorrow instead of next week.

Terry: What? (4)_____?

Adam: I know. Looks like we'll have to start studying right now.

Terry: This is (5)_____! I can't study everything for tomorrow!

Adam: Look, getting angry (6)_____. Let's just get our books and head to the library right now.

Terry: This really (7)_____.

Application Activities

Study Tip
Find a study partner. Choose 3 dialogs from the exercises in this book and act them out. Use appropriate gestures!

1. **Grammar.** Pick 1 topic and write a paragraph suggesting some possible changes and discussing their outcomes. Use *modals* and *passive modals* in your paragraph. Possible topics include improving your home, fixing problems in the city you live in, improving the city transportation system, adding interesting night life, improving your English class. For example (my city): *More student housing needs to be built. The bridge should be repaired.*

2. **Vocabulary.** Many words have both figurative and literal meanings. Pick 5 of the expression pairs from the Vocabulary section. Write 10 sentences using both the figurative and literal expressions from the unit. Can you find other pairs of figurative and literal expressions?

3. **Writing.** Choose 1 of the proverbs below. Write a paragraph to explain your interpretation. Compare your paragraph with a classmate. Do you agree on the meaning?

   - Fall 7 times, stand up 8. (from Japan)
   - Aiming isn't hitting. (from Uganda)
   - A fly does not mind dying in coconut cream. (from Tahiti)
   - A rich heart may be under a poor coat. (from Ireland)
   - Money is a good servant but an evil master. (from Mexico)

4. **Speaking.** The Spanish writer Cervantes said, "Proverbs are short sentences drawn from long experience." Tell about your favorite proverb. What is it and why do you like it? What does it mean to you?

5. **Project.** In Listening C, you hear about a person's nightmare. Describe a dream that you or someone you know has had. Research some possible meanings of this dream. Use sites on the Internet or books about dreams. Report what you found out.

Grammar Explanations

This section contains the same grammar explanations that are found on the CD-ROM. They are included here for your quick reference. To view the animated presentation, go to the Grammar section of Unit C.3 in the CD-ROM course.

Grammar 1: Future Continuous

1. We use the **future continuous** to talk about something that will be in progress at a specific time in the future.

   Dean: We'll **be practicing** this afternoon.

   When we use the future continuous, we aren't interested in when the activity will start or end. It may start before or after the specific time mentioned.

2. Remember, we usually don't use continuous forms with non-action verbs.

   We do **NOT** say: ~~Dean will be having a headache tomorrow.~~

Future continuous with *Will*

I **will** (**not**) **be playing** soccer tomorrow.

You **will** (**not**) **be playing** soccer tomorrow.

He/She/It **will** (**not**) **be playing** soccer tomorrow.

We **will** (**not**) **be playing** soccer tomorrow.

They **will** (**not**) **be playing** soccer tomorrow.

---

3. We form the future continuous with ***will be*** + the **base form** of the verb + ***-ing***.

   We often use contractions with this form.

   Tony: She will be waiting for you.
   She**'ll be waiting** for you.

   Nick: Dean will not be playing in the next game!
   Dean **won't be playing** in the next game!

4. We can also form the future continuous with ***be going to*** + ***be*** + the **base form** of the verb + ***-ing***. The meaning is the same.
   Nick **will be playing** in the next game.
   Nick **is going to be playing** in the next game.

   Remember, in conversation and informal writing, we usually use contractions with *be going to*.
   He**'s going to be playing** in the next game.
   He **isn't going to be sitting** the game **out**.

Future continuous with *Going to*

I **am** (**not**) **going to be playing** soccer tomorrow.

You **are** (**not**) **going to be playing** soccer tomorrow.

He/She/It **is** (**not**) **going to be playing** soccer tomorrow.

We **are** (**not**) **going to be playing** soccer tomorrow.

They **are** (**not**) **going to be playing** soccer tomorrow.

Grammar 2: Object Adjective Clauses

1. **Adjective clauses** (also called **relative clauses**) identify nouns or indefinite pronouns such as *one, someone*, and *something*. Adjective clauses often answer the question *Which one?* or *Which ones?*

   Nick: You're the 2 people **I wanted to see**.

   I wanted to see is an adjective clause. It identifies the 2 people. In other words, Nick wanted to see these particular people.

   Nick: You're the 2 people **I wanted to see**.

2. Adjective clauses often begin with a **relative pronoun**, such as *who* or *that*.

   The **relative pronoun** refers to a noun or pronoun outside the adjective clause. The rest of the adjective clause tells more about that noun or pronoun.

   Talia: This is the tape **that I told you about**.

   The relative pronoun is *that*. It refers to *tape*. The adjective clause is *that I told you about*. It gives information about the tape.

   Talia: This is the tape **that** I told you about.

3. The relative pronoun combines 2 sentences into 1 sentence.
   That's the video. Talia made the video.
   That's the video **that Talia made**.

4. In **object adjective clauses**, the **relative pronoun** is the **object** of the verb in the adjective clause.

   In the following sentence, the verb is *heard*. The object of the verb is *conversation*.
   Talia: We heard the **conversation**.

   The **conversation** will clear Nick's name.

   The **conversation that we heard** will clear Nick's name.

   When the sentence changes to an adjective clause, the object of the verb is the relative pronoun *that*.

   Notice that the relative pronoun **always comes first** in an adjective clause.

5. We can use the relative pronoun *who* or *that* when the object of the adjective clause is a **person**.

> **Nick:** There's **someone who I have to go see.**
> There's **someone that I have to see.**

We can also use the relative pronoun *whom* when the object is a person, but this is very formal.

> The **soccer player whom the Federation is investigating** is the very popular Nick Crawford.

6. We use the relative pronoun *that* or *which* when the object is a **thing**.

> **Nick:** My conversation wasn't the only **one that she recorded.**
> My conversation wasn't the only **one which she recorded.**

That is more common than *which* in informal conversation.

7. Relative pronouns **don't change forms**. They're the same for singular and plural objects. They're also the same for male and female subjects.

> That's the **man who I saw.**
> Those are the **women who I saw.**

8. We often **leave out the object relative pronoun**. This is very common in informal conversation and writing.

> Talia's the one **who** Nick wants to see.
> Talia's the one **Nick wants to see.**
> *Newsline* is the show **that** I always watch.
> *Newsline* is the show **I always watch.**

Grammar 3: Passive Modals

1. Verbs can have either an **active** or a **passive** form. We use the active form of a verb when we want to focus on the agent (the "doer") of the action.

> Talia **is going to interview** Nick later in the day.

The example focuses on Talia, the one who may interview Nick.

We use the **passive** form of the verb when we want to **focus on the receiver** of the action.

> Nick **is going to be interviewed by Talia** later in the day.

The example focuses on Nick.

2. All verb forms (present, past, present and past continuous, present and past perfect, etc.) can be used in the passive. We can also use **modals** in the passive. To form a passive modal, we use a **modal** + *be* + the **past participle**.

> The tape **can be edited.**

3. We use *can* with the passive to talk about **present** or **future** ability.

> **Nick:** The World Cup matches **can be seen** all over the world.

We use *could* with the passive to talk about **past ability**.

> Nick's innocence **couldn't be proven** without Talia's help.

4. We use *could, may, might*, and *can't* with the passive to talk about **future possibility** or **impossibility**.

> Dean **might be sent** to jail for framing Nick.
> The interview **may be scheduled** for later today.

5. We use *should, ought to*, and *had better* with the passive to talk about **advice**.

> **Tony:** The Soccer Federation **ought to be told** right away about Nick's innocence.

6. We use *have to* and *must* with the passive to talk about **necessity**.

> **Jackie:** The tape **had to be edited.**

C.4 Just Being Honest

🎧 **A. Listen to Track 30.** *Nick is talking with Patty. Complete the conversation.*

Patty: Oh, you know who else I see on TV a lot now? That reporter who broke the story. What's her name again? Talia something.

Nick: Talia Santos. Yeah, I heard (1)_____ a job at a different news show.

Patty: You don't look very happy about it.

Nick: Well, we've both been so busy . . . (2)_____ really hard. I (3)_____ to see her much lately. And now she's going to be moving.

Patty: It sounds like you need to speak with her.

Nick: You're right, Patty. I'll see you later.

Patty: Bye, Nick. Hey! Let me know how things turn out.

🎧 **B. Listen to Track 31.** *Nick is visiting Talia at her office. Complete the conversation.*

Nick: What I'm trying to say is, I want to (1)_____ with you. I don't want you to move.

Talia: Good. Because *this* is where I'm moving.

Nick: Huh?

Talia: *This*, this is my new office. I (2)_____ *Newsbeat* _____. Tony said he'd match their offer.

Nick: So in other words . . . I just (3)_____ of myself.

Talia: No. As usual, you were just being honest. It's one of the qualities I (4)_____ about you.

🎧 **C. Listen to Track 32.** *Match the first and second part of each person's statements.*

_d_	**1. Tony:** What you have done is to put your	**a.** a long, long time.
___	**2. Tony:** I'm really glad you're staying—I hope for	**b.** a role model for me.
___	**3. Amy:** I've always looked	**c.** happy endings.
___	**4. Amy:** You've been	**d.** heart into everything you do.
___	**5. Mrs. Santos:** Where there's a will,	**e.** there's a way.
___	**6. Mrs. Santos:** You can do anything	**f.** to know you again.
___	**7. Nick:** I got a chance	**g.** up to you.
___	**8. Nick:** Here's to you and	**h.** your heart desires.

Vocabulary

See Appendix 2 to review the vocabulary terms.

Complete each sentences with the best expression from the box. Adjust the form and tense as necessary.

break a habit	break the ice	break a law
break new ground	break the news (to somebody)	break a promise
break a record	break (somebody's) heart	

1. If people aren't talking to each other at a party, somebody has to _____. If someone tells a story or a joke, then other people will start talking.

2. Did somebody _____ to Sylvia? She's going to be laid off. They're closing down her department.

3. Ms. Boyd doesn't know it yet, but John Donnelly is taking a new job in Chicago. She really likes him a lot. I know it's going to _____.

4. Nick has scored a goal in each of the last 7 matches. If he scores a goal in the next match, he'll _____. Last year, Roberto Lamas scored 7 goals in a row, but no one has ever scored in 8 straight matches.

5. Tony says he drinks too much coffee. He wants to _____, but it's going to be hard for him to give it up.

6. Last month, *Newsline* started the first news program for children, called *News Pulse*. It's a big success. They've _____ with this type of program.

7. Amy, I'm sorry to _____! I know I said we'd go camping this weekend, but I have to work.

8. Excuse me, Officer. What did I do? Was I driving too fast? Did I _____?

Grammar 1

Adjective Clauses: Review and Expansion

A. *Jackie and another actor, Susie, are in a commercial for Glitter Toothpaste. Combine the sentence in italics with the sentence in parentheses. Create 1 sentence that has an adjective clause.*

1. **Susie:** Gee, Jackie, your teeth look great! *Your smile has a glitter and a shine.* (**You only see such a shine on television!**)

   Your smile has a glitter and a shine that you only see on television!

2. **Jackie:** They do look great! *But I remember a time a while ago.* (**My teeth were dull and yellow . . . like yours!**)

   But I remember a time when my teeth were dull and yellow . . . like yours!

3. **Jackie:** It seems like just yesterday . . . Oh, wait! *It was just yesterday.* I can see a difference already! (**I started using Glitter.**)

   It was just yesterday _____.

4. **Jackie:** *A friend of mine recommended Glitter to me.* (**My friend has beautiful teeth**).

   A friend of mine _____.

5. **Jackie:** And remember 1 thing, Susie! *Glitter is the only brand!* (**Glitter can give you the white, bright smile you've always dreamed of.**)

   _____

6. **Susie:** Glitter sounds great! *Can you tell me the name of the store?* (**You bought Glitter at this store.**)
   Can you tell me _____?

7. **Jackie:** There's no store, Susie. That's right. *The only way you can get this wonderful toothpaste is to visit our website—glittertoothpaste.com.* Our web operators are standing by. (**The toothpaste will change your life.**)

   _____

   Jackie and Susie: And remember, all that glitters is not gold!

B. *Write a few sentences about a product that you really like. Use adjective clauses with* when, where, that, which, who, *or no relative pronoun.*

EXAMPLE: I really like the hair gel that I got last week. The place where I bought it sells lots of great products at low prices. The gel has a smell which really relaxes me.

_____

_____

_____

Grammar 2

Auxiliary Verbs for Emphasis

A. *Starlight Movie Studios has decided to produce a movie called* The Nick Crawford Story. *The story will be based on the events that happened to Nick, Talia, Tony, Amy, Dean, and Jackie. The writer is talking with the actors about two possible endings for the movie. Fill in the blanks with the correct auxiliary for emphasis. Note: When we speak, we emphasize by making words longer and stronger. When we write, we underline, capitalize, or italicize emphasized words.*

Cast

Nancy Golden: writer	Nick: Nathan Crane
Amy: Amelia Brighton	Jackie: Julie Berringer
Talia: Natalie Sanders	Dean: Dana Barks
Tony: Timothy Gray	Patty: Patricia Green

1. **Nancy Golden:** Have you finished reading the script?

   Amelia Brighton: We __HAVE__ finished the script, but we'd like more time to talk about the ending.

2. **Natalie Sanders:** Larry, you _____ think ending 1 is exciting, don't you?

   Timothy Gray: Well, yes, but I _____ wish the bad guy, the Dean character, had gotten into more trouble. He deserved it. I mean, he _____ commit a crime.

3. **Amelia:** I agree. It seems that none of the criminals in the story really got punished for their actions.

   Nathan Crane: Yes, it _____ seem that way. I guess that's why I prefer ending 2.

4. **Julia Berringer:** I think ending 1 is a little depressing. The main characters, the Talia and Nick characters, don't become romantically involved at the end of the story.

   Dana Barks: No, they _____ get romantically involved. They don't get married or anything like that, but they _____ agree to spend more time together.

5. **Patricia Green:** Nancy, maybe you got too cautious at the end of the story.

   Nancy: Well, I guess I _____ get too cautious at the end. I guess I didn't want to make it a total love story.

6. **Natalie:** Maybe you could write that ending again.

   Nancy: Maybe I _____ write it again. This time, I'll include more romance.

7. **Nancy:** What do you think, Nathan? Would you like a more romantic ending?

   Nathan: Oh, yes, I _____ like that. I think the audience would like that, too.

B. *Write a short dialog in which you agree and disagree with someone's comments about a movie. Use auxiliaries for emphasis.*

Your friend: _____

You: _____

Your friend: _____

You: _____

Grammar 3

Study Tip
Review! Look back through the units. Review at least 10 of the exercises and 5 of the Application Activities.

Review of Phrasal Verbs

It's 2 years into the future! Amy and Josh are getting married. Talia, Nick, and Tony are at the wedding reception, and they are making toasts (giving speeches). Complete the conversation with the phrasal verb in parentheses. Change the object to a pronoun whenever possible.

Josh: We are now going to hear from some of our wonderful guests. Will the musicians please

(1) **(keep down / the music)** _____keep it down_____ during the toasts?

Talia: Congratulations, Josh and Amy. To be honest, when Amy and Josh first started dating, I wasn't

sure I wanted to (2) **(go along with / the idea)** _____. Actually, Amy tried

to (3) **(fix up / Talia)** _____ with Josh, but I was too busy—I could only

(4) **(think of / my work)** _____! But I'm so glad everything has (5) **(worked

out for / Josh and Amy)** _____. And now that Amy is a full-time reporter,

I would just like to say: I hope no reporting assignment ever (6) **(comes between / Amy and

Josh)** _____. Cheers!

Nick: Congratulations, Amy and Josh. It's a great reception. I'm very happy that I could (7) **(turn out

for / the reception)** _____. I know that you wanted to have the wedding

sooner, but I'm so glad that you (8) **(put off / the wedding)** _____ until

after soccer season! I guess this gave you more time to (9) **(think over / your decision)**

_____. And I know you made the right one. All the best!

Tony: It's great to be here. Amy has become a great colleague for all of us at *Newsline*. As you know,

it's so easy to (10) **(get along with / Amy)** _____. She's been so helpful to

her co-workers. She never (11) **(let down / her co-workers)** _____. You can

always (12) **(count on / Amy)** _____. She's a great person to have on your

side. And Josh, how did you get to be the lucky guy to have Amy on *your* side? Anyway—best

of luck to you!

Language Functions

See Appendix 3 to review the language function charts.

Complete the sentences with an appropriate phrase. Use the cues in parentheses.

Amy and Irene are talking about Irene's plans.

Amy: Hey, I've been (1) (*talking about intentions*) _____ to call you, but I haven't had time. What are your plans for the future?

Irene: Well, what I (2) (*talking about plans*) _____ is look for a job in New York. My brother lives there.

Amy: Oh, wow. That sounds like the perfect place for you. I hope things (3) (*wishing someone luck*) _____.

Irene: Thanks.

Chris and Talia are talking about Talia's plans.

Chris: Hey, Talia. I've been planning to call you, but things (4) (*talking about intentions*) _____. What are (5) (*asking about plans*) _____?

Talia: Well, I intend to keep working at *Newsline* for the moment. I'm hoping to get promoted there soon.

Chris: Good luck to you. (6) (*asking for updates*) _____.

Talia: I will, thanks.

Application Activities

1. **Grammar.** Look through all of the Grammar Explanations in your LEI Activity and Resource Book. Circle all the headings (for example, "Adjective Clauses"). Draw 2 circles around the headings that you need to review again. For each review point, write a short dialog that includes the grammar point.

2. **Vocabulary.** Pick 20 words and expressions from LEI 4 and make a vocabulary test with them. Try making a matching or multiple choice test. Write an answer key, too. Then exchange tests with a classmate.

3. **Writing.** Talia and Nick say that the truth always wins out, and in the story, the truth did win out. Do you agree with the idea that in life the truth always wins out? Explain and give examples.

4. **Speaking.** Ask 2 people about their future plans and share some of your plans with them. Use new expressions you've learned.

5. **Project.** The LEI story of Nick and Talia is finished. Well, Part 1 is finished. Pretend that you are a scriptwriter. Your job is to prepare a script idea for Part 2. What will happen next to Nick, Talia, Amy, Tony, Jackie, and Dean? If possible, work with a group of 2 or 3 other students. Think of several ideas and discuss them. Prepare a synopsis (summary) of your ideas for the story. What will happen at the beginning of the story? What will happen in the middle? What will happen at the end? Present your synopsis to the class.

Grammar Explanations

This section contains the same grammar explanations that are found on the CD-ROM. They are included here for your quick reference. To view the animated presentation, go to the Grammar section of Unit C.4 in the CD-ROM course.

Grammar 1: Adjective Clauses: Review and Expansion

1. Adjective clauses (also called **relative clauses**) often begin with a **relative pronoun**. The relative pronoun can be the **subject** or **object** of the adjective clause.

    Patty: Is Talia Santos the reporter **who broke the story?**

    In this example, the relative pronoun *who* is the subject of the adjective clause.

    Nick: Yes. She's the one **that I worked with.**

    In this example, the relative pronoun *that* is the object of the adjective clause.

2. We can use the relative pronouns **who** or **that** for a **person**.

    Nick: Talia's the **person who did the most to help me.**

    Talia's the **person that did the most to help me.**

    We sometimes use **whom** for a **person** when the relative pronoun is the **object** of the clause. **Whom** is very formal.

    Host: This year, the Most Valuable Player award goes to an **athlete whom we all admire.**

3. We can use the relative pronouns **that** or **which** for a **thing**.

    Talia: I turned down the **job offer that I got at** *Newsbeat.*

    I turned down the **job offer which I got at** *Newsbeat.*

    That is more common than **which** in informal conversation.

4. We use **where** in adjective clauses that describe a **place**.

    Nick: Is there **someplace where we can go for a few minutes?**

    The adjective clause *where we can go for a few minutes* describes *someplace.*

5. We use **when** or **that** in adjective clauses that describe a **time**.

    Patty: It seems as if it was just **yesterday when you asked me to turn up the volume.**

    It seems as if it was just **yesterday that you asked me to turn up the volume.**

    The adjective clause *when you asked me to turn up the volume* (or *that you asked me to turn up the volume*) describes *yesterday.*

6. In adjective clauses, we often **leave out the object relative pronoun**. We also leave out **when** or **that** in adjective clauses that describe a time. This is very common in informal conversation and writing.

There's something **that** I need to discuss with you.
There's something **I need to discuss with you.**

It's hard to find a time **when** we can talk.
It's hard to find a time **we can talk.**

We can't leave out *where.*
That's the juice bar **where Nick Crawford liked to go.**

We do **NOT** say: ~~That's the juice bar Nick Crawford liked to go.~~

Grammar 2: Auxiliary Verbs for Emphasis

1. We often use **auxiliary verbs** for **emphasis**—to give something special importance. Auxiliary verbs include the verbs *do, be,* and *have,* and modals like *can, could, should,* and *will.*

    Talia: A lot of people didn't believe Nick, but he **was** telling the truth!

2. If the sentence already has an auxiliary verb, we emphasize it by putting more **stress** on it when we speak. When we put stress on a word, we make it longer and stronger.

    Patty: Hey, Nick. You should see this commercial.
    Nick: I **have** seen it.

    Amy: Did you know that Talia was offered a job in Chicago?
    Nick: No, I **didn't** know that.

3. If the sentence does not have an auxiliary verb, we use the auxiliary **do, does,** or **did** for emphasis. Notice that the base form of the verb always follows *do, does,* or *did.*

    Josh: Too bad you don't like soccer.
    Amy: I **do like** soccer.

    Patty: It seems like just yesterday.
    Nick: It **does seem** like yesterday.

    Nick: I guess things worked out for Jackie.
    Patty: And for you, too. You scored the winning goal.
    And for you, too. You **did score** the winning goal.

4. If the main verb in the sentence is *be,* we can emphasize it in the same way.

    Talia: Nick **was** innocent.

5. We emphasize things for many different reasons. One reason is to **agree** with something someone has said.

    Patty: It seems like it was just yesterday when you asked me to turn up the volume.
    Nick: Yeah, in a way it **does seem** like just yesterday.

We also use emphasis when we **disagree** with something.

> **John:** It's too bad that Talia is moving to Chicago.
>
> **Amy:** She **isn't** moving to Chicago. She's staying at *Newsline*!

Grammar 3: Review of Phrasal Verbs

1. **Phrasal verbs** are verbs that have 2 parts—a **verb** + a **particle**.

    > **Turn out** is a phrasal verb. *Turn* is the verb; *out* is the particle.

    The particle looks just like a preposition, but it is actually 1 part of this 2-part verb. The particle often changes the meaning of the verb.

    > **Patty:** Let me know how things **turn out**.

    In the example, *turn out* means *have a particular result.* As you can see, the verb *turn* plus the particle *out* has a completely different meaning from the verb *turn* by itself.

2. Some phrasal verbs are **inseparable**. This means that the 2 parts—verb and particle—always stay together. When an inseparable phrasal verb has an object, the object always comes after the 2 parts of the verb.

    > **Amy:** What do you **think of the commercial**?
    >
    > **Talia:** What do I **think of it**? I think it's ridiculous.

    In the conversation, the noun *the commercial* and the pronoun *it* are objects of the verb *think of.* Both noun and pronoun objects always come **after** an inseparable phrasal verb.

    We do **NOT** say: ~~What do I think it of?~~

3. Some phrasal verbs are used with certain prepositions when they have an object. We sometimes call these combinations **3-part verbs**. 3-part verbs are **inseparable**.

    > **Patty:** Things have **worked out for you**, Nick.

    The phrasal verb *work out* means *stop being a problem.* We use it with the preposition *for* when there is an object.

    We don't use the preposition when there is no object.

    > **Nick:** Yes, they have **worked out**.

4. Many phrasal verbs are separable. This means that the noun object can come either after or between the 2 parts of the verb.

    > **Talia:** I **turned down the job**.
    >
    > I **turned the job down**.

5. When the object of a separable phrasal verb is a **pronoun** (a word like *him, her,* or *it*), it must go between the verb and the particle.

    > **Nick:** Why did you **turn down the job**?
    >
    > **Talia:** I turned down the job because I didn't want to move.
    >
    > **Talia:** I **turned it down** because I didn't want to move.

    We do **NOT** say: ~~I turned down it.~~

6. Remember, we use phrasal verbs a lot, especially in conversation. Phrasal verbs are often more common than their definitions. For example,

    > **Mark:** I **ran into** my cousin yesterday.

    is more common than

    > **Mark:** I **met** my cousin **by accident** yesterday.

Phrasal Verb	Definition
run into	meet by accident
turn up	make louder
keep on	continue

Appendix 1: Audioscript

Unit A.1

Track 1

Nick: Right. So she meets me in the lobby, we shake hands, and she takes me to lunch.

Talia: Yes, to a little place around the corner, as I recall.

Nick: Right. And then she asks me to endorse a new pair of shoes.

Talia: Yeah. You told me. They're called Kicks.

Nick: Right. And she explains that I'll have to wear the shoes when I play. And the company will use my name in ads.

Track 2

Jackie: So, you'll wear our shoes when you play. And we'll use your name in ads. Do that and $50,000 is yours.

Nick: Sounds good. And this will be sometime next year?

Jackie: Uh, yeah, that's right. We can work out the details later for this, but we'll probably want you to appear in a commercial.

Track 3

Commercial 1: Tropica Tours

Picture this—You're on a quiet, breathtakingly beautiful beach. The sky is a cloudless blue. The warm waves of the ocean peacefully wash over the shore; a gentle breeze caresses your face. Now, you and that special someone begin strolling leisurely along the edge of the sparkling water, your feet sinking softly into the silky white sand. You feel calm, relaxed, totally content . . . without a care in the world. Tropica Tours . . . for faraway places close to home.

Commercial 2: Silver Mountain

Picture this—It's a bright and glorious day, sun directly overhead. Majestic white peaks are all around you, kissing the clear blue sky. You glide along alone, at one with the snow-covered trail, your breath and the whoosh-whoosh of your skis in perfect harmony. Silver Mountain . . . cross-country skiing at its peak.

Commercial 3: Globaltrek.com

Picture this—You set out at dawn, with the mist still hugging the mountain. Now, at mid-morning, the sun has burned through. The lush meadow flowers sparkle in the light. Beauty is all around you, and your heart delights as you hike along the winding trails. All you can think is, "It doesn't get better than this." Globaltrek.com . . . we'll take you there.

Unit A.2

Track 4

Talia: Tony, I need to see you. I have to bring you up to date on the Nick Crawford story.

Tony: Come in. What's going on?

Talia: I just spoke to Nick. He was tricked. The tape was edited. He didn't take a bribe. It just sounds that way.

Tony: Well, what does your audio expert say?

Talia: I forgot to tell you. It's definitely Nick's voice. And he said that the tape was definitely edited.

Tony: But I don't get it. Who's behind this?

Talia: One of Nick's teammates, Dean Bishop. He resents being in Nick's shadow. He wants to be the only star on the team.

Tony: Of course! The bottom line is . . . being the star is worth a lot of money in endorsements.

Talia: Still. I can't imagine . . .

Tony: OK. So, now, what's your plan?

Talia: I have an idea. I need some help from Amy.

Tony: Fine. You can have another day on this and we won't run the story yet. But one more thing, Talia, I hope you're not emotionally involved in this story.

Talia: Me? Emotionally involved?

Tony: I know you want to clear Nick's name. But if you want to have a career in journalism, you have to remember to stay objective.

Track 5

Patty: Hi there. What can I get for you?

Amy: How about a large iced tea?

Patty: Coming right up.

Amy: . . . and a little information?

Patty: What kind of information?

Amy: I'm trying to get hold of someone named Jackie Bishop. I was told that she's a member of this club.

Patty: Hmm. She used to be, but not anymore. She stopped coming here a while ago. Maybe a year ago, even.

Amy: Oh. Too bad.

Patty: Her brother Dean, the soccer player, works out here, though. I remember seeing him yesterday, around lunchtime. Maybe you could speak to him.

Amy: Actually, I'd rather avoid seeing him. It's a little complicated between him and me, if you know what I mean.

Patty: Oh, I see. Well, here's an idea. I think Jackie's taking acting classes over at the university. Maybe you could catch up with her there.

Amy: She's taking acting classes at the university?
Patty: Mmm-hmm.
Amy: Ah . . . Yes . . . That's a great idea. Thanks for the tip.
Patty: Oh, likewise! Thanks!

Track 6

Welcome to the customer service department. If you want to be successful in this job, you have to remember a few basic guidelines in answering customer calls. Always keep in mind that this is a customer service department, which really means that 90% of your calls will be complaints.

First and foremost, don't take any complaint personally. The caller is complaining about service from the company, *not* from you personally. So don't take any complaint as a personal attack on you.

Second, get the details, and take good notes. Find out *exactly* what the customer is complaining about. Ask specific questions like, "What exactly happened? When did it happen? Where were you? What exactly did the person say to you?" and so on.

Third, and this should be obvious, don't sound like you're blaming the customer for any mistake or error.

Fourth, be sure to *confirm* the information about the customer's complaint exactly, verbatim if possible. Don't write a general summary of the complaint. OK?

Next, fifth, tell the customer you know how he or she feels. In other words, be sure to sympathize with the customer. Say things like, "Oh, you must feel terrible," or "If I were in that situation, I would be very angry, too," or "I'm really sorry you've had this problem." Sometimes, just this step alone will help them feel better.

Sixth, be sure to listen to the customers' needs. Don't assume you know what they need or what they want you to do. Ask very directly, "What would you like me to do for you?"

And seventh, don't give them advice. Don't say, "You should do this or you should do that." Instead, give the customers their options. Say something like, "In this situation, here are your options. You can do this . . ." or "you can do that . . . ," or "I can do this for you," or even "what would you like me to do?"

And finally, eighth, at the end of each call, be sure to use the customer's name and thank the customer for calling. You know, you can say something like, "Ms. Jones, I appreciate your calling, and thank you for your patience." Then wait for the customer to hang up phone to end the call. You should never be the one to end the call first.

Unit A.3

Track 7

Amy: Talia, are you almost here?
Talia: I'm about 10 minutes away. Can you see her?
Amy: Yes. She's sitting on a sofa. Hurry up. Classes start in about 20 minutes.

Talia: Well, just go over to her and start a conversation. You've done your homework, haven't you?
Amy: My homework?
Talia: I mean, have you found out what courses she's taking, and everything?
Amy: Oh, yeah. I can do a little acting myself, if that's what you mean.
Talia: So go act like a drama student, and go and talk to her. I'll be right there.

Amy: Excuse me. You're in the drama program, right?
Jackie: Yes! Oh, hi.
Amy: Do you know if Professor Roberts is teaching this semester?
Jackie: Yes, he is. He's fabulous. I'm in his improvisation class. In fact, it's tonight.
Amy: Oh, great.
Jackie: I've been taking classes here for about a year and I think he's been my best teacher.
Amy: I know what you mean. He's very . . . inspiring.
Jackie: Yes, absolutely. I've become a much better actor since I started taking his classes . . .
Amy: Yes, I'm sure you have.

Track 8

Amy: Oh, I'm Amy Lee, by the way.
Jackie: Hi. I'm Jackie Bishop. Well, that's my real name. My stage name is Jackie Baker.
Amy: So, do you have an agent?
Jackie: As a matter of fact, I spoke to an agent last week. I just sent him a tape, and he thought it was incredible.
Amy: I'm not surprised. You do seem . . . incredible.

Track 9

So you want to register for classes this semester? OK. Here's what you'll need to do.

Since you're a full-time student, you first need to go to the Administration Building and go to the Student Accounting Office. At the Student Accounting Office, go to the "undergraduate student accounts" window and show them your student ID. They'll verify that your tuition and fees are up to date and give you a green "clear" form. That means that your account is clear. That's what you've got to do first.

Next, take the "clear" form to the Student Union Building and go to Student Advising. Ask to see a course adviser . . . show your "clear" form to the course adviser . . . and then he or she will look up your intake form and give you a pink printout of classes that you're eligible for. That pink form is called your "A list"—that means your authorized list, or classes that you're authorized to take. OK? You can only register for the classes on your "A list."

Then you need to go to the Dixon Building and go to Registration with your green "clear" form and your pink "A list." Then sit down at one of the computers, log on, enter your Student ID number, and follow the onscreen directions. OK? And by the way, you might want to hurry. A few thousand students will be registering for classes this week.

Track 10

Talia: Gee, you look so familiar.

Jackie: Really? We might have seen each other around campus.

Talia: I guess so. Or we may have been in a class together. I'm taking journalism classes.

Jackie: No, it couldn't have been a class. I'm taking acting classes, like Amy.

Talia: Oh, well. I'll probably think of it later.

Jackie: Speaking of classes, I'd better run. I don't want to be late for Professor Roberts.

Talia: Hold it. I think I remember where I've seen you.

Jackie: Really?

Talia: Yes. The Gower Building.

Track 11

Talia: So what did you find out?

Amy: Listen to this. Jackie and Dean are going to Valentino's after her class tonight to celebrate. She's booked a special table.

Talia: This is perfect. Great work. You should be proud of yourself.

Amy: Thanks, but it was nothing. Piece of cake, in fact.

Track 12

Caller 1

Reservations: Hello, this is La Scala. May I help you?

Woman 1: Yes, I need to make a reservation, please.

Reservations: For when, ma'am?

Woman 1: For tonight, around 7:15 . . . no, make that 7:30.

Reservations: Certainly, let me check what's available . . . how many are in your party?

Woman 1: It's, um, 2, just 2.

Reservations: Yes, we have a table . . . on the terrace or in the garden room. Which do you prefer?

Woman 1: The terrace, please.

Reservations: And your name, please?

Woman 1: Please put the reservation under the name Gould, G-O-U-L-D.

Reservations: Very well, ma'am. That's Gould, party of 2 . . . on the terrace, for 7:30 this evening . . . We look forward to seeing you.

Caller 2

Reservations: Hello, La Scala reservations. Can I help you?

Man: Hello . . . Yes, I'd like to reserve a table for tonight . . .

Reservations: How many in your party, sir?

Man: Party of 6.

Reservations: Party of 6, ah . . . for this evening?

Man: Yes, for this evening . . . around 7:00 or 7:30 . . .

Reservations: Actually, sir, the earliest I have a table for 6 is, let's see, 8:30 . . . Is that all right?

Man: Um, yes, that'd be fine.

Reservations: And it will be in the garden room . . .

Man: Yes, OK . . .

Reservations: Could I have the name of the party, please?

Man: Jackson, J-A-C-K-S-O-N.

Reservations: Very good, Mr. Jackson. We'll expect you this evening at 8:30 . . . for the garden room . . .

Caller 3

Reservations: Hello, La Scala.

Woman 2: Hello, Paolo.

Reservations: Ah, Ms. Desmond, how wonderful to hear your voice . . . And what can I help you with today?

Woman 2: I need a table for this evening.

Reservations: Certainly, Ms. Desmond. For what time, please?

Woman 2: 8, as usual.

Reservations: Excellent. 8 o'clock. And how many in your party this evening?

Woman 2: There will be 4 of us.

Reservations: Excellent. And would you like a table in the main dining room or would you prefer to be in the garden room this evening?

Woman 2: In the main dining room would be preferable, thank you.

Reservations: Absolutely. We'll see you this evening, Ms. Desmond.

Woman 2: Thank you, Paolo.

Reservations: Ciao.

Track 13

Talia: Oh, thank goodness you got my message!

Nick: Yeah. What's going on?

Talia: Don't worry. I'm not trying to get you to take me out on a date. I'm trying to help you save your career.

Nick: Oh, that. Yeah, right, I almost forgot.

Talia: Be serious. I care about . . . I care about your future.

Nick: So do I!

Talia: Good—you wore a tie.

Nick: Yeah, your message said, wear a tie and a jacket. You look nice, by the way.

Talia: Thanks. So do you. . . . So, as I was saying, I have a feeling Dean and Jackie are going to talk about you as soon as they get here.

Track 14

Warning sounds. We respond to these sounds very naturally without thinking. Our natural response to warning sounds is a feeling of "alarm." When we hear a warning sound, like a dog growling or a burglar alarm, we have an instinctive, physical response.

Low-frequency warning sounds, like a cough, cause us to "freeze," that is, to stop and not approach further. They actually produce a "freeze" reflex in our stomach and our legs. So when a car beeps its horn, pedestrians look out and stop crossing the street. When the warning buzzer sounds in a game show, the contestants have to stop playing. And when a ship blows its fog horn, other ships are warned to keep out of its way.

High-frequency warning sounds, like a smoke alarm, on the other hand, warn you to "seek." They actually produce a signal in our brain to open our eyes and ears and turn our heads. When you hear a referee's whistle in a sports match, you turn to see what's happening. When you hear the siren of an ambulance, you try to see where the ambulance is coming from. And if you hear someone scream, it's natural to look for the person in distress to see if you can help.

So these are the two kinds of warning sounds you hear around you. Next time you hear a warning sound, pay attention to your reflexes and notice how your body naturally reacts to these sounds.

Unit B.2

Track 15

Jackie: So this woman—Amy—and I were talking when a friend of hers showed up. Then, when Amy introduced us, her friend said I looked familiar.

Dean: So?

Jackie: So, then she asked me if I worked for Kicks Shoes!

Dean: There is no Kicks Shoes.

Jackie: I know that, and you know that, but she doesn't . . .

Dean: How does she know about . . .

Jackie: I'm scared, Dean. She works for *Newsline*.

Track 16

Jackie: Speaking of which, when are you going to introduce me to Byron Walters?

Dean: Byron Walters?

Jackie: Yes, that film director friend of yours? Remember? The director who's going to make me a star!!

Dean: Oh, him . . .

Jackie: You said to be patient, but this is getting ridiculous.

Dean: Uh, I forgot to tell you. There is no Byron Walters. He quit the business.

Jackie: But he was going to give me my big break, the break that's going to make me a star.

Track 17

You know Robert, my boyfriend, right? Well, did I ever tell you about the way that Robert and I met? No? Well, it was kind of a bizarre coincidence . . . I was at a party, about 2 years ago . . . it was in New York at a mutual friend's house . . . a guy named Bassam . . . and Bassam introduced me to Robert. Bassam knew we were both from Michigan, and when he introduced us, he said, "You know, both of you guys are from Michigan." And so Robert and I started chatting, and I asked him where in Michigan he was from

. . . and he said, "Plymouth, that's near Detroit" . . . and I said, "Sure I know Plymouth, I'm from Detroit" . . . and he said, "Really? You're from Detroit? I went to high school in Detroit, Mumford High School" . . . and I said, "You're kidding! You went to Mumford High School?! My grandmother used to live across the street from Mumford High School and when I was in high school, I had to go to my grandma's house, like once a week, after school to help her out . . . and, you know, I used to watch the Mumford High School guys practicing soccer . . . the field was right across from her house" . . . and he sort of squinted at me and said, "Wait a minute . . . I was a soccer player in high school . . . " and we sort of looked at each other, like "No way" . . . and we both kind of simultaneously asked, "What year?" and he said he was there from 1992 to 1996 and graduated in '96 . . . which was exactly the year that I graduated . . . and now—get this—he suddenly asks me, "This is weird, but did you used to have long hair . . . and you used to sit on the doorstep, right?, in front of this red brick house?" . . . and I had this, like, shiver up and down my spine, and I said . . . "Yeah, yeah, that was me!" And he said, "You know, I used to see you there . . . I bet you didn't know that, did you?" And I just kind of freaked out, like what a coincidence! So, we sort of thought, you know, wow, we must be meant for each other or something, and we were kind of attracted to each other, and we started going out together, and we've been together since that night at the party. So just last Saturday, we went out for a romantic dinner at this restaurant Robert picked out called—guess what?—Mumfords—and he asked me to marry him! and . . . of course, I said, you know, "Yes."

Unit B.3

Track 18

Nick: I can't believe it! . . . They admitted everything!

Talia: And we got it all on tape.

Nick: How did you know they were going to talk about me?

Talia: I saw Jackie's face when I mentioned Kicks Shoes. I knew she would tell Dean about it as soon as she could.

Nick: This is fantastic. I'm so relieved. I was beginning to think it was all over for me.

Talia: Are you ready to go? If we leave now, we'll still be able to catch Tony.

Nick: Look, Talia. The news has already been on. There's nothing we can do to change it . . .

Talia: Yeah, I guess you're right.

Nick: Why don't we finish dinner?

Talia: . . . But if we leave now, Tony will still be in the office.

Nick: Look, Talia. This whole thing is about to be cleared up. Why don't we just take a little time now to enjoy ourselves?

Talia: Of course. You're right. Sorry, Nick. And besides, this *is* Valentino's. And I *am* with a star!

Nick: I have a confession to make.

Talia: What? You have a confession to make? I thought this whole thing was over.

Nick: No, no. It's not about that. It's about . . . well, us.

Talia: Us? Us, as in you and me?

Nick: Yes. Do you remember that class we took together in college?

Talia: Of course, I remember it. I remember it well.

Nick: And do you remember when we were studying together in the library . . .

Talia: You mean when we were studying for that Shakespeare exam?

Nick: Well, I . . . uh . . . I wanted to ask you out.

Talia: You did? Wow! . . . So, why didn't you?

Nick: I'd heard you had a boyfriend.

Talia: Oh, no! Well, I had a boyfriend, but we split up during that semester. In fact, we had split up by mid-semester.

Nick: You're kidding. I didn't know. Well, I guess I should've . . .

Talia: I'm not seeing anyone now, though, you know.

Nick: Well, then . . .

Waiter: *Tutto bene*? Is everything all right? May I get you uh, *un cafè*? *Tè*? *Cappuccino*?

Talia: I'll have a cappuccino.

Nick: Two.

Track 19

Do you remember your first day of school? Do you recall the time you met your best friend? Do you remember the last time you saw your grandfather? Of course, you do. We all recollect important events and people in our lives, thousands and thousands of events and people. But how does the memory actually work? And how accurate is our memory?

Now, most people think that the memory is like a video recorder that records every event accurately and stores it intact, like a videotape on a shelf. Then years later, when we remember something, we just replay the tape—and presto!—our memories of those events are perfectly clear. All the sights, sounds, and so on are replayed accurately. Well, this may be a logical way to think about memory, but actually, research on human memory has shown that our memories really aren't like video recordings at all.

No, instead, our memories are a combination of several mental processes. Our memories are constructed out of images from the original event, plus our emotions, beliefs, imagination, dreams, and the many things we have heard or read since that time. For example, when we think we are remembering a major event like our first day of high school or a job interview, we are actually reconstructing the event, adding to it or altering it as a result of all these different mental processes.

And our memories—unlike video recordings—change over time. They're not the same from day to day or year to year, because the connections in our brain change constantly. Our memories are also influenced by the situation and the people around us. When you're talking to one of your parents at home, you will remember

something one way; if you are talking with a close friend at school, you'll remember it differently.

So, the next time you recall an event, remember: Your memories are never really a true video recording of what happened. They're always enhanced—and altered—versions of the event.

Unit B.4

Track 20

Talia: I'm too late, right? You already aired the story about Nick on the evening news?

Tony: No, I decided not to. When I hadn't heard from you, I decided to wait.

Talia: Oh, gosh, what a relief.

Tony: As a matter of fact, I was just going to call you.

Talia: Well, I'm so glad you waited, Tony . . . Tah-dah!

Tony: So that's the tape?

Talia: Yup. This is the tape that will get Nick's name cleared.

Tony: OK. Let's hear it. I have a tape player here somewhere.

Amy: So, tell me. Tell me.

Talia: It was perfect. I got it all on tape. Jackie said that she had posed as a Kicks executive . . .

Amy: No!

Talia: Yes! And they both admitted that there was no Kicks!

Amy: Get out of here!

Talia: And Dean actually said that he had sent the tape to us . . .

Amy: Unbelievable!

Talia: Wait till you hear them. Hearing is believing! . . . Here it is, the tape that will get Nick reinstated on the team . . . Just a minute. I must not have rewound it . . . OK, now listen . . . What's going on? Is this tape player working?

Tony: It's been working just fine. In fact, I just had it cleaned last week.

Amy: Try another tape and see if that works.

Tony: Thanks, Amy. I was just about to try that.

Amy: Did you check that the recording light was on?

Talia: I was going to check it after I sat down but too much was going on.

Track 21

News Story 1

Parts of the county were hit by a devastating tornado today. More than 100 people were injured across the area and thousands more have lost power. The tornado was an F5, the most powerful, according to a preliminary measurement by the National Weather Service. In one section alone, the twister destroyed 16 houses and left a track of damage 24 miles long and 400 yards wide. Under the Fujita scale, a twister with an F5 rating has winds from 261 mph to 318 mph. The county has never had an F5 and only two F4s are on record—including one in 1926. For more information about the tornado and to see pictures of the area, go to our website and click on the tornado link.

News Story 2

Baby Barbara, the 2-year-old daughter of Christopher and Dawn Sattler, is reported to be doing well after 12-hour liver transplant surgery. Dad Christopher donated part of his liver to replace the baby's failing organ and is also reported to be in stable condition. According to Dr. Michael Gaies, the surgeon who operated on both of the patients, Christopher's own liver will regenerate itself in a matter of weeks. The prognosis for Baby Barbara is excellent. For more information about liver transplant surgery, click on our website and go to the link on Baby Barbara.

News Story 3

Rock star Peter McEnery, 51, one of the original members of the Fab Five, was married last night at his castle in Ireland to model Teresa Furfaro, 24. The two met last year while McEnery was on holiday in Italy. This is McEnery's second marriage. He has 4 children from his previous marriage, all of whom attended the wedding, along with 300 of the couple's closest friends and relatives. For more details, including the bride and groom's official wedding picture, go to our website and click on the wedding link.

Unit C.1

Track 22

Talia: I feel awful. If I had been more careful, we would have had the evidence!

Nick: Wow! And we were supposed to be *celebrating* tonight.

Talia: How stupid! I can't believe I didn't press the right buttons! I just wish I had been more careful.

Nick: And I wish you would stop kicking yourself.

Talia: Well, I'm supposed to be a professional! And I want to be a reporter! . . . I wish I could go back and do it over.

Nick: Well, you can't. Take it from me. I'm an athlete. I know. You just have to forget what's done and go on.

Talia: You're right. What's done is done. Or in this case, what's not done is done.

Nick: Look, Talia, if you hadn't done such a good job of covering the story, we never would have known the truth.

Talia: How can you stay so positive?

Nick: I don't know. It's just my nature.

Track 23

1. I enjoy life. I am a spontaneous person and I like to act according to how I feel.
2. I feel that my personal life and my professional life are improving all the time.
3. I want to contribute something to the world.

4. When people around me are feeling down, I usually try to get them to cheer up and look at the bright side of things.
5. I enjoy giving compliments and telling people how important they are to me.
6. I don't let difficulties and unfortunate events stop me from reaching my goals.
7. I worry a lot that people I am close to will leave me, even though there is usually no reason to believe that.
8. If my boss phones me and says that she wants to talk to me in person, I assume it's some bad news.
9. When I wake up in the middle of the night with a stomachache, I usually think it'll pass.
10. When I see a glass filled halfway, I usually think it's . . .

Unit C.2

Track 24

Jackie: It's amazing how easily you can get people's addresses these days. Oh, hello, Nick! Remember me?

Nick: I certainly do.

Talia: What are you doing here?

Jackie: Do you have a video camera?

Talia: Yes.

Jackie: Do you want a great story? One that will make us all really famous?

Talia: What's the catch?

Jackie: No catch. Just one small condition. If Nick agrees not to press charges against me, I'll tell the whole truth.

Track 25

Jackie: You have to understand. Dean and I had been planning this for a long time. I posed as the VP of marketing from this phony shoe company . . .

Talia: Kicks.

Jackie: Right. Kicks Shoes. Cute name, don't you think? Anyway, I knew Nick usually went to the juice bar at the health club, and I met him there.

Talia: And then?

Jackie: Then, posing as this woman from Kicks, I invited Nick to come to my office to discuss an endorsement.

Talia: And did he?

Jackie: Well, I didn't really have an office, you know. So I met him in the Gower Building lobby and took him to lunch. I recorded the whole conversation. Dean took over from there. He doctored the tape to make it sound like Nick had accepted a bribe.

Talia: Why did you decide to tell the truth now?

Jackie: Dean promised to introduce me to some big-shot movie director, and I believed him. Well, I just found out that Dean had been lying the whole time.

Track 26

DV: My guest this evening is the well-known talk-show host, Charlene Flowers. We're very pleased to have you, Charlene. Thank you for joining us.

CF: Well, thank you for having me, David.

DV: Charlene, I wonder if you would share some of your secrets for what makes a successful interview.

CF: Actually, David, an interview has four phases. There's the preparation phase, then the opening, then the heart of the interview, and finally the closing.

DV: OK, then, let's see, preparation comes first. That makes sense. So how exactly do you prepare?

CF: Well, I basically want to build a solid foundation for any topics we're going to talk about, so I do research. I read recent articles about the person and try to talk to a few people who know him or her personally. Of course, I try to review the person's new work ahead of time, like if they've just written a new book or done a new movie.

DV: Um-hmm. And during your preparation, do you write things down . . . or what do you do?

CF: Actually, I do take a few notes, yes, but mostly I try to get a feel for what the person is about . . . their motivations, passions . . . you know, I want to find out what makes the person tick.

DV: And after your preparation, what's next? Do you talk with your guest before the actual TV interview?

CF: Oh, no, never. I want it to be fresh, spontaneous. The opening, when the guest first comes on . . . the first 2 minutes . . . is essential. This is the time to build rapport . . .

DV: And how do you go about building rapport?

CF: I always begin with something personal—I talk about some way the person I'm interviewing has affected *me*. That helps me make a personal connection with my guest. If it's appropriate, I introduce some humor or levity. I really want to help the guest relax and open up. After a few minutes, I make the transition to the heart of the interview.

DV: What do you mean by the "heart of the interview"?

CF: The heart of the interview is where I can get to the goals of the interview. In each interview, I try to explore a few key areas. So I have to keep my goals in mind all the time.

DV: Do you have specific questions that you write down in advance?

CF: Oh no, no, never. . . . But I do constantly keep in mind what the key areas are.

DV: Uh-huh. And how do you introduce these key areas?

CF: Well, I might say, "I've read that such-and-such happened to you . . . tell us more about that . . ." and then I just let the guest talk. I may ask open-ended questions to probe a little further, but mostly I let the guest talk.

DV: And do you give your personal reactions to what they say?

CF: Mmm . . . not really . . . I don't judge their views as right or wrong . . . I just want to keep them talking and to reveal more . . .

DV: And how about the closing for the interview?

CF: Ah, the closing . . . is also very important because I want the guest to feel good about opening up and connecting with me. So the closing is when you express appreciation for the interview. I always shake hands and thank the guest for the interview . . . and I often end by suggesting that they come back soon.

DV: Well, Charlene, thank you for sharing some of your techniques with us. . . . We have to take a break, we'll be right back . . .

Unit C.3

Track 27

Nick: Dean! And Coach! You're just the two people I wanted to see.

Dean: Nick! Sorry, man, tough break. But you know what they say, "Don't do the crime if you can't do the time."

Nick: Dean, that's the smartest thing I've ever heard you say.

Coach: Nick, are you going to be OK?

Nick: You bet! I've got something I want to show you both.

Jackie: My brother heard that Nick had gotten rid of his agent. So I went and offered Nick $50,000 to endorse a pair of shoes. I was very convincing, if I must say so myself. Anyway, Nick agreed and I got it all on tape. Of course, the tape had to be edited to make it sound like Nick was accepting a bribe, but Dean took care of that.

Dean: That lying . . .

Nick: Dean, I'd keep quiet if I were you. Jackie gave us hard evidence. It turns out my conversation with her was not the only one she recorded.

Dean: This is crazy!

Coach: I don't know what to say. I'm so sorry you had to go through all of this.

Nick: Thanks, Coach.

Coach: Well, I think this is all over now. We'll be starting practice in an hour—you'll be there, right?

Nick: Oh, sure! But I might be late. There's someone I have to go talk to.

Track 28

Amy: You must be very happy.

Nick: I really am. My name has been cleared. I'm really relieved. This has been a nightmare!

Tony: Now that the truth has come out, how about giving *Newsline* an exclusive interview?

Nick: That depends.

Tony: Ah, depends on what?

Nick: I will talk to *Newsline* as long as my favorite reporter gets to do the interview.

Tony: Oh, you must mean Talia.

Amy: Of course he does!

Tony: Go ahead. Just remember . . . Don't let your emotions get in the way of your job.

Nick: Just one more thing. Can we schedule the interview for later? I've got to go to soccer practice now.

Tony: No problem. Talia will be waiting for you.

Track 29

I've been having this recurring nightmare, but last night it ended differently. In this dream, I find myself walking down a winding path in the forest, and it's getting dark, and I start to feel lost, like where am I? How did I get here? And then I see this wolf, out of the corner of my eye, a really scary wolf. And I think, oh no, this wolf—he's following me. And I run ahead through the forest. And then I wake up, my heart beating fast. But last night, when the dream happened, this time I didn't wake up, I just kept going.

And now I'm on this wide, empty stage, and I look out into the audience, and there are all these people I know and some figures I can't make out so clearly — but everyone is looking at me . . . and I realize that they're waiting for me to perform . . . like in a play or something . . . and I go back behind the stage and I see this red velvet cape, but I don't put it on, and I come back out on the stage, and everybody's looking at me, so I just go down to the edge of the stage and start singing this beautiful song . . . and I'm like, wow, is this my voice? And I finish my song, and everyone in the audience starts applauding, very warmly, and I go down into the crowd and start shaking hands with everyone . . . and then I come to this one figure, and it's the wolf . . . just looking into my eyes . . . and this time I'm not afraid of it . . . and I just pat it on the head . . .

Unit C.4

Track 30

Patty: Oh, you know who else I see on TV a lot now? That reporter who broke the story. What's her name again? Talia something.

Nick: Talia Santos. Yeah, I heard she's been offered a job at a different news show.

Patty: You don't look very happy about it.

Nick: Well, we've both been so busy . . . she's been working really hard. I haven't had a chance to see her much lately. And now she's going to be moving.

Patty: It sounds like you need to speak with her.

Nick: You're right, Patty. I'll see you later.

Patty: Bye, Nick. Hey! Let me know how things turn out.

Track 31

Nick: What I'm trying to say is, I want to spend more time with you. I don't want you to move.

Talia: Good. Because *this* is where I'm moving.

Nick: Huh?

Talia: *This*, this is my new office. I turned *Newsbeat* down. Tony said he'd match their offer.

Nick: So in other words . . . I just made a fool of myself.

Talia: No. As usual, you were just being honest. It's one of the qualities I like most about you.

Track 32

Tony: I just want to say, well done, Talia. You've been a great researcher, and I know you're going to be a top-notch reporter. You know, I always tell you not to let your emotions get in the way of your job. What you have done is to put your heart into everything you do. I'm really glad you're staying—I hope for a long, long time.

Talia: Thanks, Tony. I really appreciate it.

Amy: I guess it's my turn. Hey, Talia, I just want to say congratulations on your promotion. You really deserve it. You know, I've always looked up to you. You've been a role model for me. And now that you've been promoted to a reporter, I'm going to work even harder . . . so I can continue to follow in your footsteps.

Talia: Thanks, Amy. Just remember, if you want to follow in my footsteps, wear comfortable shoes!

Tony: Just make sure they're not Kicks Shoes!

Amy: And we're also happy to have with us a special guest, Mrs. Santos . . .

Mrs. Santos: Good evening everyone. Thanks, Amy, for inviting me, and congratulations to you, too. It has been wonderful meeting all of you. Talia is very lucky to have such great people to work with. Talia, I am so proud of you . . . you've always made me so proud . . . and as I've told you at least a thousand times: Where there's a will, there's a way. I guess I don't have to keep telling you *that* anymore! I know you'll always keep your eye on your goals. So, congratulations, sweetheart. You can do anything your heart desires.

Talia: Thank you, Mom. I love you.

Amy: Wow, that is so sweet. And now Nick.

Nick: Talia, you know, I'm an optimist, but there were times when even I wondered if my story was going to have a happy ending. Well, it had three happy endings: first, my career in soccer is doing great; second, Talia, you've got a new career as a reporter; and third—and most important for me—I got a chance to know you again. I know you'll be a great reporter. Here's to you and happy endings.

Talia: Oh, thank you, Nick . . .

Appendix 2: Vocabulary Terms

Unit A.1

accurate *adj.* correct or exact
These figures aren't very accurate. Can you check them again?

attractive *adj.* pretty, beautiful, or pleasant to look at
He's a very attractive man. He should be a model.

dependent *adj.* needing something or someone to help or support you
Children are usually dependent upon their parents until they become adults.

legal *adj.* allowed by the law
Voting is legal in the United States for people over the age of 18.

likely *adj.* probably, or almost certainly
It is likely to snow tomorrow, so wear your winter coat.

original *adj.* new and different
He has an original idea for a new product.

practical *adj.* sensible and likely to succeed or be effective
I'm sure her proposal will work—it's very practical, though it isn't very creative.

regular *adj.* happening or being repeated at the same times
We have a regular meeting every Friday.

sane *adj.* able to think and act in a normal and reasonable way
The only sane way to get around a big city is by public transportation.

suitable *adj.* right or acceptable for a particular purpose
Let's buy this toy for the baby. The label says that it's suitable for small children.

Unit A.2

along the same lines *idiom* something that is similar to what another person is talking about
Everyone had such a great time at your party last month that we decided to do something along the same lines for our party.

be out of line *idiom* behave badly or in a way that is not acceptable in a particular situation
She was out of line to yell at poor Antonio when he made a mistake.

down the line *idiom* at a future time
Maybe 5 years down the line I'll start my own business.

drop someone a line *idiom* to write and send a short letter to someone
Please drop me a line when you get back.

get a line on something *idiom* to get information about someone or something so you can understand it or them better
I'm trying to get a line on the hotels before we go there for our vacation.

give someone a line *idiom* to tell someone something that isn't true so they will do what you want
The salesman gave us a line about how perfect his product was.

lay it on the line *idiom* to tell someone the truth in a very direct way
Our teacher laid it on the line and said we wouldn't pass the course if we didn't study harder.

read between the lines *idiom* to be able to understand the full meaning of something, even though you have not been given all the details
He said he was happy with his job, but reading between the lines, I could tell that something was wrong.

take a hard line *idiom* to be determined to make people behave in the way that you want and unwilling to change your opinions [often used in business and politics]
Since Floretta became principal, she has taken a hard line with the teachers. Now they really have to work.

the bottom line *idiom* used to tell someone what you think the most important part of a situation is [This idiom comes from business accounts in which the bottom line is the final line that shows how much profit a company has made or how much money was lost.]
The bottom line is that we have to finish the report by Friday afternoon.

Unit A.3

agent *n.* someone who is paid by actors or musicians to find work for them
My agent got me a part in the new play.

cameraperson *n.* a person who operates a camera to film movies or television programs
The movie is beautifully filmed. The cameraperson did a great job.

costume designer *n.* someone whose job is to make patterns for actors' clothes for movies or plays
The costume designer did a wonderful job creating the clothes for the play.

film director *n.* a person who tells the actors and other people what to do when a movie is being made
Alfred Hitchcock was a film director who was famous for his mysteries.

makeup artist *n.* a person who puts things on the faces of actors to improve or change their appearance
It took several hours for the makeup artist to make the actor look like an ape.

producer *n.* someone who controls the preparation of a play or a movie but does not direct the actors
He was the producer of several hit plays on Broadway.

scriptwriter *n.* someone who writes what the actors have to say in a play or movie
The actor read the lines that the scriptwriter gave him.

set designer *n.* a person who designs the place where a movie is filmed or a play is acted
The background created by the set designer looked very realistic to the audience.

sound engineer *n.* someone who controls what people hear in a movie
The sound engineer had a difficult time preparing the television program about earthquakes.

stuntperson *n.* someone who takes the place of an actor when something dangerous has to be done in a movie
Special effects done by computer can sometimes take the place of a stuntperson.

Unit A.4

a piece of cake *idiom* something that is very easy
Getting there is a piece of cake—it's just a 10-minute walk.

a rotten apple *idiom* someone who is dishonest and has a bad effect on others
It only takes 1 rotten apple to give the whole industry a bad name.

a smart cookie *idiom* someone who is intelligent and confident
Fumihito is a smart cookie; it won't take him long to learn the new program.

beef something up *phr. v.* to improve something, especially to make it stronger or more interesting
After a number of bank robberies, we decided to beef up security.

butter someone up *phr. v.* say nice things so someone will do what you want
You really need her help, so butter her up and she may agree to give you a hand.

go bananas *idiom* (*informal*) to become very angry or excited
He'll go bananas if you forget his birthday again.

have egg on your face *idiom* to be embarrassed or seem stupid because of something you did or said
She has egg on her face after what she said at the press conference.

pie in the sky *idiom* an idea or plan that you think will never happen
The city's plans for a new stadium are just pie in the sky.

small potatoes *idiom* something that is not very important
Her little business was small potatoes compared to Kalgoorie's huge corporation.

sour grapes *idiom* a bad attitude that makes people criticize what they can't have
She said Bob shouldn't have gotten a raise, but that was just sour grapes because the boss didn't give her one.

Unit B.1

bald *adj.* having little or no hair on your head
My father has been bald since he was 40.

braid *n.* a length of hair that has been separated into three parts and then woven together
Sun-Mi likes wearing her hair in a braid.

cornrows *n.* a way of arranging hair in which it is put into small, tight braids along the head
It took a long time to do Sharon's hair in cornrows.

crew cut *n.* a very short hair style for men
In some countries, soldiers get crew cuts when they join the army.

curly *adj.* having a lot of curls
Erika is the girl with the curly blonde hair.

kinky *adj.* kinky hair has a lot of tight curls
My hair is just a little curly, but my son's is really kinky.

ponytail *n.* hair tied together at the back of your head
Makiko's hair is so long that it's easy for her to make a ponytail.

straight *adj.* hair without curls
The little Chinese girl had short, straight, black hair.

wavy *adj.* hair that grows in loose curls
They hired a woman with long, wavy hair to do the shampoo ad.

wig *n.* a covering of hair that you wear on your head
Milan wore a blonde wig to disguise himself.

Unit B.2

keep back *phr. v.* used to tell someone to not stand near something or not move toward it
The police officers told the people on the street to keep back from the accident.

keep going *collocation* (*spoken*) used to encourage someone who is doing something and to tell them to continue
Keep going, Hicham, you're going to break the record!

keep it down *phr. v.* (*spoken*) used to ask someone to make less noise
Ask the kids to keep it down—I'm on the phone.

keep out of something *phr. v.* to not get involved in a situation
Matti was one of those people who seemed unable to keep out of trouble.

keep quiet *collocation* (*spoken*) to not say anything in order to avoid complaining, telling a secret, or causing problems
We knew what they were doing was wrong, but we kept quiet.

keep someone guessing *idiom* to make it difficult for someone to know what you are going to do next
A great chess player always keeps his opponent guessing.

keep someone posted *idiom* to continue giving someone information about a situation that he or she is interested in
I asked Yumi to keep us posted, but we haven't heard from her yet.

keep the change *collocation* (*spoken*) used when paying someone, to tell them they can keep the extra money you have given them
Mary was grateful to the taxi driver for giving her information about the city, so she told him to keep the change.

keep to the subject *collocation* to talk or write only about the subject you are supposed to be talking about
I know that you'd prefer to talk about other things, but please keep to the subject.

keep your shirt on *idiom* (*spoken*) used to tell someone to be calm and patient
Keep your shirt on—we have plenty of time before the flight leaves

Unit B.3

ask someone out *phr. v.* to ask someone to go to a restaurant, film, etc. with you, especially because you want to start a romantic relationship with them
He wanted to ask her out, but he was too shy.

be in a serious relationship *collocation* to be in a romantic relationship that is meant to continue for a long time
I don't think they're in a serious relationship. They've only been dating for a month.

be on the rebound *collocation* to be upset or confused because a romantic relationship you had has ended
When you're on the rebound, it's easy to make bad decisions, so be careful!

be seeing somebody *collocation* to be having a romantic relationship with someone
Is Padam still seeing Margo?

fix somebody up *phr. v.* (*informal*) to provide a suitable partner for someone to meet in a romantic way or have a romantic relationship with
If you want, I can fix you up with a date for the party.

go on a blind date *collocation* to have an arranged meeting between a man and a woman who have not met each other before
I went on a blind date, and I was pretty nervous about going out with someone I hadn't even met.

have a crush on somebody *collocation* to have a feeling of romantic love for someone, especially for someone you do not know very well, used especially about feelings that teenagers have
I had a terrible crush on Mel Gibson when I was in high school.

play hard to get *idiom* to try to make it difficult for someone to have a romantic relationship with you
Mary seems unfriendly, but she's just playing hard to get.

play the field *idiom* to have many different romantic relationships
Renato gave up playing the field when he finally decided to get married.

split up *phr. v.* if two people split up, they end their romantic relationship or marriage
Glenda and Keith were always arguing, so they finally decided to split up.

Unit B.4

clear a debt *collocation* to get rid of a debt by paying all the money you owe
You'll need to clear your debt before we can loan you any more money.

clear a space *collocation* to move things so there is room for something else
Before you put that down, let me clear a space on the desk.

clear someone's name *collocation* to show that a person is not guilty of something
Marthe worked hard to clear her father's name.

clear something with someone *collocation* to get official permission for something to be done
The ambassador cleared it with the State Department before making the announcement that he was leaving the country.

clear the air *idiom* to do something in order to end an argument or bad situation
Fernando tried to clear the air by asking Marlise why she was angry.

clear the decks *idiom* to get ready to start doing something new, by finishing work, dealing with problems, or clearing things away
Shu decided to clear the decks of old projects before going on to something new.

clear the table *collocation* to take off the used plates, forks, etc. after you have eaten
Nguyen and I will clear the table if you help with the dishes.

clear the way *collocation* make it possible for something to happen
Their phone conversation cleared the way for the contract.

clear your head *collocation* to stop worrying or thinking about something
When I'm studying for a test, I sometimes go for a walk to clear my head.

clear your throat *collocation* to cough in order to speak with a clear voice
The speaker took a drink of water and cleared her throat before continuing.

Unit C.1

overbook *v.* to sell more tickets for a theater, airplane, etc. than there are seats available
Our flight was overbooked, so we had to wait 3 hours for the next one.

overcharge *v.* to charge someone too much money for something
The store overcharged me for the coat, but I didn't realize it until I got home. I'd like a refund.

overcome *v.* to succeed in controlling a feeling or problem
It was really hard for Gyorgy to overcome his fear of flying.

overdo *v.* to do or use too much of something
When jogging, you have to be careful not to overdo it.

overeat *v.* to eat too much, or more than is healthy
Sisiphong overate at the dinner and had a terrible stomachache that night.

overestimate *v.* to think something is larger, more expensive, or more important than it really is
She overestimated how many children would come to the party and had a lot of cake and ice cream left over.

overhear *v.* to hear by accident what other people are saying when they do not know that you are listening
Giullietta knows about her promotion. She overheard us talking about it at lunch.

overlap *v.* if two events or activities overlap, the first one finishes after the second one starts
My trip to Italy overlaps with the first week of the school semester.

overlook *v.* to not notice something or to not realize how important it is
The accountant was careless and overlooked a number of items in the budget.

overreact *v.* to react to something with too much anger or surprise, or by doing more than is necessary
When Patrick made a little joke about Miki's boyfriend, she overreacted and got really angry.

oversee *v.* to watch a group of workers to be sure that a piece of work is done correctly
Ms. Mardziuk will oversee the project and make sure that the workers do a good job.

Unit C.2

come about *phr.v.* to happen or develop
Changes in company policy have come about gradually as the market has grown.

come across *phr.v.* to meet someone or discover something, usually by chance
Marpessa came across the picture of her former classmate while reading a magazine.

come between *phr.v.* to spoil the relationship between two or more people, by causing problems or arguments
My parents don't like Mpholo, and I'm afraid he's coming between us.

come by *phr.v.* to visit someone for a short time before going somewhere else
Fernanda came by to see us before she went to visit her grandparents.

come down to *phr.v.* if a problem or difficult situation comes down to something, that is the most important point or idea to consider
It all comes down to being able to get a loan when you're buying a car.

come down with *phr.v.* to become sick with a particular illness
When I was on vacation, I came down with a bad cold.

come forward *phr.v.* to offer to help someone in an official position with a crime or problem
Several witnesses came forward to help the police with their investigation.

come out *phr.v.* to become known after being hidden
Yesterday it came out that the mayor had received a bribe for awarding the contract.

come through *phr.v.* to continue to live, exist, be strong, or succeed after a difficult or dangerous time
Robert lost a lot of money when the economy was bad, but he managed to come through it and build up his business again.

come up *phr.v.* to be mentioned or suggested
That proposal came up at the last meeting.

Unit C.3

catch a ball *v. phr.* to get hold of and stop a ball that is moving through the air
Leon wanted to be on the baseball team, but he never could learn to catch a ball.

catch someone's eye *idiom* to make someone notice someone or something
The picture in her office caught my eye.

hot temper *n.* someone who has a hot temper becomes angry very easily
I know my father loved us, but he had a hot temper, and we were always a little afraid of him.

hot water *n.* water with a high temperature
It's not a good idea to wash cotton clothes in hot water because they may shrink.

loud color *n.* a color that is too bright
Monique's taste in clothes is very conservative, but her sister prefers loud colors, like orange and red.

loud noise *n.* a lot of sound
I was awakened by a loud noise coming from the apartment above.

smooth surface *n.* a smooth surface is completely even, without any bumps
Sometimes the ice on the lake did not have a very smooth surface, so skating was a bit difficult.

smooth talker *n.* someone who is good at persuading people and saying nice things, but who is not trusted
Ellen was a smooth talker, and she was the best saleswoman in the store.

soft pillow *n.* a cloth bag filled with very soft material that you put your head on when you sleep
I sleep better on a hard mattress, but I like soft pillows.

soft rock *n.* a type of rock music that does not have a strong beat and that includes many songs about love
There was a soft rock group at the concert last night.

steal a car *v. phr.* to take a car that belongs to someone else without his/her permission, and not give it back
While Uri was in Los Angeles, someone stole his car.

steal a look *v. phr.* to look at someone or something quickly and secretly
She couldn't resist stealing a look at the movie star sitting at the next table.

thin curtain *n.* a large piece of hanging cloth, covering a window, that can easily be seen through
I was always uncomfortable with those thin curtains because the neighbors could look right into our house.

thin excuse *n.* an excuse that is not good enough to persuade you that it is true
When Sylvie was late for the third time in a week, she made a thin excuse about missing her bus.

throw a ball *v. phr.* to make a ball move quickly from your hand through the air by moving your arm
I was throwing a ball to my son when I accidentally broke the window.

throw a fit *idiom (spoken)* to get very angry and upset
Dad will throw a fit if you don't wash the car.

tired joke *n.* something that you say to make people laugh but that is boring because it is too familiar
Please don't tell that tired joke again tonight—our guests have heard it at least a dozen times!

tired worker *n.* someone who has been working hard and feels like resting or sleeping
The farmer felt sorry for his tired workers after a hard day in the hot field, so he gave them the next day off.

warm weather *n.* when the temperature is slightly hot and other conditions are nice
Another cold, gloomy day—I wish we'd have some warm weather again!

warm welcome *n.* a greeting that is friendly in a way that makes you feel comfortable
Ebbe was nervous about having dinner at his boss's home, but a warm welcome at the door made him relax.

Unit C.4

break a habit *collocation* to stop doing something that you have done regularly for a long time
It took a long time for Joao to break the habit of staying up until 2 a.m. after doing it for so many years.

break a law *collocation* to disobey a law
The judge decided that Roscoe had broken the law.

break a promise *collocation* to not do what you have promised to do
Everyone expects politicians to break their promises to the voters.

break a record *collocation* to do something faster or better than it has ever been done before
She broke the world record for the 10,000 meters by more than 50 seconds.

break a story *collocation* to make a story known for the first time
Nightly News was the first program to break the story about the company's financial problems.

break a sweat *collocation* to start sweating, especially because you are working or exercising hard
When we were jogging, it only took about 10 minutes before I broke a sweat.

break new ground *idiom* to do something completely new that no one has ever done before
The car manufacturer broke new ground with its award-winning safety features.

break somebody's heart *idiom* to make someone very unhappy by ending a relationship with them
It broke Sharmila's heart when Vilayat told her he didn't want to see her anymore.

break the ice *idiom* to say something to make someone you have just met less nervous
To break the ice, the leader of our tour group asked us all to introduce ourselves.

break the news to somebody *collocation* to tell someone about something bad that has happened
I hated breaking the news to the kids that our vacation plans had been canceled.

Appendix 3: Language Functions

Unit A.1

Opening	Catching Up on Things	
Hi, So, Say, Hey, Um,	what's happening what's going on what's up what's the story	with the reports?

Linking Back	Additional Information
Also, As I was saying, By the way, And another thing,	I thought the meeting went really well.
To get back to the meeting, Oh, about the meeting,	I thought it went well.

Changing the Subject	New Topic
By the way, Incidentally, Before I forget, Oh, I keep meaning to tell you, In case you didn't know, Oh, I wanted to tell you, I don't mean to change the subject, but	I'm going to be in late tomorrow.

Unit A.2

Asking about Problems

You	look	depressed. upset. worried. a little down.	Are you OK? Is anything wrong? Is everything all right? What's the matter?
	seem		
	sound	like you've got a problem.	What happened?

(Unit A.2 charts continue on next page.)

Talking about Problems

Talking about the Situation

It's my boss. She doesn't like me.

It's my class. It's too difficult.

Talking about Feelings

I've got a problem with	my job.
I'm stressed out about	this report.
I'm worried about	our budget.
I'm upset about	my class.
I'm nervous about	

Suggesting a Solution

I've got an idea. Here's an idea. I know!	Your teacher can probably help. Why don't you talk to him?
Maybe you could If I were you, I'd	talk to your boss. give him a call.
Why don't you	leave tonight?

Responses

That's a great idea.	Hmmm . . . that might work.
That's a thought!	I can't do that.
You're right.	I'd rather not do that.
I guess you're right.	No, that won't work.

Unit A.3

Asking for General Impressions

What do you think of What's your impression of What's your take on How was	Professor Martin? your meeting with Josh? Sam's report? Valentinos' restaurant?
Tell me about	the movie you saw. Nick Crawford.

Asking for Specific Impressions

What do you like about What's so special about What didn't you like about What was so great about	Professor Martin's lectures? Velentino's restaurant? Tony's presentation? your boyfriend?

Responding to Questions about Impressions

Positive

He's Her lectures are The actors were	fabulous. super. superb. great. wonderful. very inspiring. the best! really interesting. absolutely amazing.

Neutral		Negative	
She's It's	all right. so-so. OK. not bad.	The singer was The food was	kind of dull. a little boring. not too great. pretty bad.

Unit A.4

Making Closing Comments

(Well,)	It was great seeing you.
	It's been nice talking to you.
	Look at the time! Sorry I have to rush off like this.
	It's getting late. I really should be going.
	I've got to run.
	I have to go now.
	I won't take up any more of your time.

Suggesting Keeping in Touch

Give me a call sometime.

We ought to get together soon.

Let's keep in touch.

Let's do this again soon.

Confirming the Next Meeting

| I'll | see you at the office | tomorrow. |
| | catch you in class | next week. |

Saying Good-bye

Bye!	See you later.
Take care!	So long.
Catch you later.	Take it easy.

Unit B.1

Compliments about Appearance (of people or things)

You look great today.

Your haircut looks great—it really suits you.

Nice sweater!

That's a cool pair of earrings.

I really like the way you've decorated your room.

What a beautiful painting!

Compliments about Achievements

Great job!

Way to go! You really played well today.

That was delicious. My compliments on a great meal.

Compliments about Abilities

You're so smart!

Wow! You're a great cook.

Hey, you're really good at playing the piano.

Complimenting on Specific Achievements at Work

I thought you	handled those questions really well.
	did a great job on the report.
	gave a fantastic presentation.
I'd like to compliment you on	your report.
	your presentation.
	the way you handled yourself today.
I read your report.	Great job!
	Well done!
I saw your presentation.	Excellent work!
	Keep up the good work!

(Unit B.1 charts continue on next page.)

Accepting the Compliment	Agreeing with the Evaluation
Thanks. I appreciate it. Thanks for the compliment. That's so nice of you to say. I'm glad you think so.	I like it, too. (*appearance of thing*) I thought it went well, too. (*achievement*)
	Adding Information
	I bought this last week. (*appearance of thing*) Well, I did my best. (*achievement*) I learned how to do that in a class. (*ability*)

Downplaying
Oh, this old thing? It's nothing special. (*appearance of thing*)
I didn't really play all that well. But thanks. (*achievement*)
It wasn't much, really. (*achievement*)
Oh, no, it wasn't that good. (*achievement*)
Me, a great cook? You must be joking. (*ability*)

Unit B.2

Interrupting	
But . . . Well, I think . . . No, I don't think so . . . Wait a minute . . .	you're wrong about that!
What?!	You're wrong about that!
Asking Someone Not to Interrupt You	
Please don't interrupt me. Will you let me finish? Can I finish, please? If you'll just let me finish . . . Excuse me. I'm still talking.	

Statement	Expressing Disagreement
Dean is our best player.	I don't know about that. I hate to disagree with you, but . . . I don't think so. That's nonsense! You've got to be kidding!
	Showing Skepticism/Sarcasm
	Hah! Yeah, yeah . . . Yeah, right . . . Whatever!

Conceding to Someone	
Yeah, you may be right.	OK, whatever you say.
I suppose that's true.	Oh, well, it doesn't really matter.
I see your point, I guess.	Well, let's not fight about this.

Unit B.3

Reminding about Past Events

Do you remember when we Remember when we Do you recall the time we	went to the championship game together?
I was just thinking about when we	went on that trip to California.
Do you recall	having that class together in college?

Commenting about Memories

Positive/Neutral

I remember that well. That was a great class. That was a lot of fun, wasn't it?	We had a great time, didn't we? Sure, I remember. How could I forget?

Negative

Oh, don't remind me.
What a nightmare that was!

Expressing Regret

I wish I had I should have I guess I should have	worked harder.
I really wanted to I missed my chance to	ask you out.
I'll always regret	not taking that class.

Unit B.4

Identifying a Problem

Identifying a Problem	Calm Response
Something's wrong with the TV. The TV doesn't work. I can't get the TV to work. This TV is acting up. The TV is messed up. The TV is broken. There's no sound.	That isn't so bad. That's not a big deal. I know what's wrong. **Emotional Response** Oh, no! This is a disaster. What are we going to do?!

Suggesting a Course of Action

Did you check	the batteries?
Have you tried	replacing the batteries? using another tape?
Maybe we need to What we ought to do is	replace the batteries. press the "record" button.
Why don't we	use another tape?

(Unit B.4 charts continue on next page.)

Suggesting a Course of Action	Responding
Did you check the batteries?	Yes, I checked them.
	Yes, I've tried that.
	Yes, I did that already.
Maybe you need to replace the batteries.	I don't think that will work.

Suggesting a Course of Action	Responding	Committing to a Course of Action
Did you check the batteries?	No, maybe that's what's wrong.	I'll do it now.
	No, I guess I should do that.	I'll give that a try.
	I was going to, but I forgot.	Let's do that.
	That never crossed my mind.	Let's give that a try.
Maybe you need to replace the batteries.	OK.	Let's try that now.
	Good idea.	
	You're probably right.	

Unit C.1

Blaming Yourself	
It's all my fault!	I'm so ashamed!
I blew it!	I should have been more careful.
I've made a terrible mistake!	
I can't believe I did that!	How could I have let this happen?
What an idiot I am!	

Blaming Someone Else	
How could this have happened!?	That was really stupid of them!
What did she do that for?	He should have been more careful.
It's all his fault!	
How could she do this?	She shouldn't have let that happen.
I can't believe you did that!	

Comforting Someone	Responding
Calm down.	OK, I guess I should.
Take it easy.	
You're overreacting.	Maybe you're right.
Don't be so hard on yourself.	I guess you're right.
Stop beating yourself up.	
It's not that bad.	Yeah, maybe I'm overreacting.
What's done is done.	I know. But I still feel bad.
There's nothing you can do about it now.	
Don't worry about it. You did your best.	

Unit C.2

Expressing Enthusiasm	
I can't wait It's going to be great	to start my new job.
I'm really looking forward to I'm so excited about	meeting Nick tonight.

Statement Expressing Emotion	Sympathetic Response
I'm really looking forward to meeting him.	I bet. I can imagine. Of course you are. I would be, too. I know what you mean.
I'm not really looking forward to going there.	I can understand that. I know what you mean. I don't blame you. I wouldn't be either.

Expressing Reluctance	
I'm not too thrilled about I'm not too excited about	going to the conference.
I wish I didn't have to Actually, I really don't want to	go to the conference.

Expressing Worry	
I'm kind of worried about I feel a little funny about	going to the conference.

Expressing Apathy
I'm not really up for it. To tell the truth, I couldn't care less about it.

Unit C.3

Statement	Showing Anger
Sorry, but I can't let you in.	How dare you?! This is ridiculous! This is unbelievable! I can't believe that! This is an outrage! That's outrageous! You can't be serious! What!? *Colloquial* That ticks me off! That really burns me up! Thanks a lot! *Crude* This stinks!

Calming Someone Down	
Calm down. Take it easy.	Don't let it get to you. Don't get so upset. Keep cool! These things happen. Maybe you're being a little too sensitive about this. Getting angry won't do any good.

Unit C.4

Talking about Intentions

I've been meaning to		but things keep coming up.
I've been planning to	call you,	but I haven't had time.
I've been wanting to		but I keep forgetting.

Wishing Someone Luck	Asking for Updates
Good luck.	Let me know what happens.
Best of luck to you.	Let me know how things turn out.
I hope things turn out well for you.	Let me know how everything goes.
I'm sure everything will work out.	Keep me posted.
	Keep in touch.

Asking about Plans

What are you planning to do?

What are you going to be doing after this?

Do you have any plans for the future?

What are your plans?

Talking about Plans

I hope to get	
I may just get	
I intend to get	a job.
What I plan to do is get	
I'm thinking of getting	

Answer Key

Unit A.1

Listening

A. 2. shake   5. endorse   8. play
3. takes   6. explains   9. will use
4. asks   7. wear

B. 1. 'll wear   5. is
2. play   6. can work out
3. 'll use   7. want
4. Do

C.

	Tropica Tours	Silver Mountain	Globaltrek.com
cloudless blue	✓		
bright and glorious		✓	
majestic white		✓	
hugging the mountain			✓
caresses your face	✓		
perfect harmony		✓	
strolling leisurely	✓		
sparkle in the light			✓
heart delights			✓
totally content	✓		

Vocabulary

A.

un-	im-	in-	il-	ir-
unbelievable	impractical	incredible	illegal	irregular
unsuitable		independent		
unattractive		insane		
unlikely		inaccurate		
unoriginal				

B. 2. unlikely   5. insane   8. practical
3. original   6. independent   9. attractive
4. impractical   7. likely   10. illegal

Grammar 1

2. started   8. want
3. was developing   9. tastes
4. was   10. has come up with / came up with
5. decided
6. has always been   11. is running / will run
7. is

Grammar 2

A. 1. aren't you; I am; aren't you
2. don't you; I don't
3. is he
4. haven't you; I haven't
5. Didn't he say
6. Aren't you dating; I'm not

B. Sample question:
Star: Harrison Ford
Your question: You've been in a lot of action movies, haven't you?

Grammar 3

A. 2. to get   4. her to take
3. him to give   5. to take

BONUS
Each person changed the information a little bit. Everyone changed the name of the director and changed his "promise" of a part to Jackie.

B. Sample answers:
1. My girlfriend wants me to move to her city.
2. I convinced my parents to buy me a computer.

Language Functions

1. What's the story / What's going on / What's happening
2. to get back to the article / about the article / as I was saying
3. I wanted to tell you / By the way / Before I forget / Oh, I keep meaning to tell you

Unit A.2

Listening

A. 2. I forgot to tell you.
3. He resents being in Nick's shadow.
4. He wants to be the only star on the team.
5. I know you want clear Nick's name . . .
6. If you want to have a career . . .
7. You have to remember to stay objective . . .
8. I'm trying to get hold of someone . . .
9. She stopped coming here a while ago . . .
10. I remember seeing him . . .
11. I'd rather avoid seeing him . . .

B. 1. sympathizing   6. giving . . . options
2. finding out   7. giving . . . options
3. using   8. bad
4. sympathizing   9. good
5. taking . . . personally

Vocabulary

Email 1: drop you a line; down the line

Email 2: take a hard line; along the same lines

Email 3: giving me a line; was out of line

Email 4: lay it on the line; get a line on

Grammar 1

A. **2.** In 1999, the Tower **was** visited by a million people.
3. Because of wars in Italy, workers ~~were~~ stopped construction on the Tower several times.
4. In 1995, 600 tons of lead ~~is~~ **was / were** added to the Tower.
5. In 1178, people ~~were~~ noticed that the Tower was tilted.
6. In 1273, the architect Pontedera ~~was~~ realized that the tower couldn't be straightened.
7. In 1990, the Italian government ~~was~~ closed the Tower to the public.
8. In 2001, the Leaning Tower of Pisa **was** reopened by the government.

BONUS
Sample answer:
Toshogu Shrine is a famous place. It is located near my hometown, Wakayama. The shrine was built 400 years ago. Inside there are several large paintings. They were painted by Jingoro Hidari, a famous artist.

Grammar 2

A. **1.** words; vocabulary
2. help; problems
3. drink; tea
4. information; questions
5. money; dollars

B.
NC advice	NC information	NC music
NC baggage	NC knowledge	C song
NC education	NC love	NC time
NC experience	NC loyalty	NC vocabulary
C idea	C minute	NC work

Grammar 3

2. to put on
3. playing
4. to pretend / pretending
5. to talk / talking; talking
6. performing / to perform
7. to be; sharing / to share
8. to watch; to attend
9. competing

BONUS
Sample answers:
1. I remember starting school for the first time.
2. I forget bumping my head on the table when I was 3.
3. I remember eating bananas all the time when I was 5.
4. I forget getting lost in a department store.

Language Functions

Sample answers:
1. You seem upset. / You look a little down.
2. Is anything wrong? / Is everything all right?
3. I'm stressed out about / I'm worried about
4. Here's an idea / I know.
5. Maybe you could / If I were you, I'd
6. That's a great idea / That's a thought!
7. You look like you've got a problem. / You seem worried.
8. I'm worried about / I've got a problem with
9. Why don't you / Maybe you could
10. I'd rather not do that. / I can't do that.

Unit A.3

Listening

A. **2.** have you found out
3. I've been taking
4. I've become
5. have

B. **1.** by the way
2. real name
3. stage name
4. agent
5. sent
6. tape
7. incredible
8. not surprised

C.
register	means	need
go	take	log on
show	ask	enter
verify	look up	hurry

Vocabulary

A.
Compound word	Two separate words
cameraperson	costume designer
scriptwriter	film director
stuntperson	makeup artist
	set designer

Ends in *-er*	Ends in *-or*
costume designer	film director
producer	
scriptwriter	
set designer	

B. **2.** set designer
3. stuntperson
4. agent
5. cameraperson
6. costume designer
7. film director
8. makeup artist
9. producer

Grammar 1

A. **2.** 've been watching; have been discussing
3. hasn't touched
4. 's eaten
5. 's been working on
6. 's been living
7. has dated
8. 's been smiling
9. 's been
10. Has . . . been listening
11. 've been shouting
12. 's been

B. Sample answers:
1. I've been living in the United States for 2 years.
2. I've played the trumpet since I was 5.
3. I've been reading a very good novel these days.

Grammar 2

2. Sometimes a casting director wants to know <u>if you understand the character.</u>
3. The director may ask you to improvise to see <u>if you are able to develop a natural feeling for the character.</u>
4. You might ask how <u>you can know what to say.</u>
5. When you have discovered who <u>the character really is</u>, you will know how <u>the character behaves.</u>
6. I wonder <u>if anyone in the class would like to try it.</u>

Grammar 3

A.
2. irrita<u>ting</u>
3. interes<u>ted</u>
4. satisf<u>ying</u>
5. ama<u>zing</u>
6. embarras<u>sed</u>
7. disappoint<u>ed</u>
8. frighten<u>ed</u>; excit<u>ed</u>

B. Sample answers:
1. *Life Is Beautiful* is a very touching film. I was inspired by the main character's sense of humor in a horrifying situation.
2. I was really frightened by the movie *The Ring*. It was terrifying!

Language Functions

2. What's so special about
3. What's your take on
4. all right

Unit A.4

Listening

A.
2. may have been
3. couldn't have been
4. I'd better
5. I've seen

B.
1. after
2. celebrate
3. perfect
4. proud of yourself
5. cake

C. *Caller 1*
5 And your name, please?
3 How many are in your party?
4 Which do you prefer?
1 May I help you?
2 For when, ma'am?

Caller 2
2 How many in your party, sir?
5 Could I have the name of the party, please?
4 Is that all right?
1 Can I help you?
3 For this evening?

Caller 3
2 For what time, please?
3 And how many in your party this evening?
1 And what can I help you with today?
4 And would you like a table in the main dining room . . . ?

Vocabulary

A.
2. butter
3. potatoes
4. grapes
5. cake
6. pie
7. bananas
8. egg
9. cookie
10. apple

B.
1. beef up my grade point average
2. a smart cookie
3. a piece of cake
4. went bananas
5. was small potatoes

Grammar 1

2. must need
3. might not be; may be; might be
4. must be; looks
5. can't be; doesn't believe
6. Could that be; that's
7. can't be
8. probably realized / may have realized; can't be / must not be

Grammar 2

2. Tony and his wife, Elisa, encourage <u>each other</u> to eat healthy food.
3. Jackie wanted to celebrate something with Dean. So she bought herself an expensive new necklace and she bought <u>him</u> a new watch.
4. Nick, Talia, and Miguel were classmates at the university. They haven't kept in touch with <u>each other</u> until just recently.
5. Coach Haskins is forgetful. He often has to remind <u>himself</u> to recharge his cell phone each night.
6. Dean talked to Brian and Hyung about Nick. He convinced <u>them</u> to avoid Nick until Nick could prove himself innocent.
7. Claire and Ryan, you've just finished a big project. Aren't you going to give <u>yourselves</u> a break?
8. Nick is disappointed in <u>himself</u> for being tricked. "How could I do this to myself?" he keeps asking.
9. We don't like to eat lunch by <u>ourselves</u>. Please join us.

Grammar 3

2. must have enjoyed
3. must not have eaten
4. must not have slept
5. may have decided
6. Could . . . have seen / couldn't have seen
7. must have known

Language Functions

1. Give me a call sometime.
2. It was great seeing you, too.
   I'll catch you in class tomorrow.
3. Well, I won't take up any more of your time.
   Let's do this again soon.

Unit B.1

Listening

A. 2. help you save
3. So do I!
4. So do you.
5. are going to talk about

B. 1. thinking
2. alarm
3. cough
4. freeze
5. siren
6. seek

Vocabulary

A.

Adjective	Noun		
	One-word noun		Two-word noun
	Noun	Compound noun	
1. bald	**6.** braid	**8.** cornrows	**10.** crew cut
2. curly	**7.** wig	**9.** ponytail	
3. kinky			
4. straight			
5. wavy			

B. 1. wavy
2. ponytail
3. cornrows
4. curly
5. crew cut
6. bald
7. straight
8. braid
9. kinky
10. wig

Grammar 1

A. 2. let; have
3. had; send
4. get; to hire
5. made; cancel
6. doesn't let; do

B. 2. A, C   3. A, C, D

Grammar 2

2. Neither can I
3. neither have Tad and Ryan
4. So do I
5. So did mine
6. So would I

Grammar 3

2. By the time she gets
3. a large party will be taking place
4. After Jamie puts on
5. While Jamie is
6. When she finds
7. she is going to take
8. as soon as she opens
9. before Pringle's security guards arrive
10. until the guards enter the room
11. After Jamie leaves
12. a helicopter will be waiting

Language Functions

2. Well, I did my best.
3. Honey, way to go! You're a really great actress.

Unit B.2

Listening

A. 1. were talking
2. showed up
3. if I worked
4. How does she know

B. 1. who's going to make me
2. to be patient
3. he was going to give me

C. 1. T
2. T
3. T
4. F
5. F
6. F
7. NI
8. F
9. F
10. T

Vocabulary

2. Keep . . . shirt on
3. keep . . . the subject
4. keep it down
5. keep you posted
6. keep . . . out of

Grammar 1

A. 2. T; T   3. T; F   4. T; F   5. F; T

B. 2. When Nick saw Dean, he coughed to warn Talia. / Nick coughed to warn Talia when he saw Dean.
3. When Jackie sat down, Dean asked her why she didn't answer her phone.
Not acceptable because it's confusing: ~~Dean asked Jackie why she didn't answer her phone when she sat down.~~
4. When Dean kept interrupting Jackie, she became very angry. / Jackie became very angry when Dean kept interrupting her.
5. When Dean told Jackie about Byron Walters, she threatened him. / Jackie threatened Dean when he told her about Byron Walters.

Grammar 2

A. 3. Talia warned Claire not to drink the milk because it was sour.
4. Dean challenged Nick to prove that he framed him.
5. Tony reminded his research staff to hand in their background research by the end of the day.
6. Dean told his dog not to chew on his new shoes.
7. Amy invited Talia to watch a movie with her and Josh at her apartment the following day.
8. Jackie warned her classmate not to be late in the future because Dr. Roberts doesn't tolerate it.

B. Sample answers:
1. My teacher told me to speak English as often as possible.
My teacher said to speak English as often as possible.
2. My friends told me to come to the movies.
My friends said to come to the movies.

Grammar 3

A. **2.** "Angel-Napped" is the *Newsline* story that's about a kidnapped baby.
3. Wraps is a small company that's owned by Talia's friend Mandy.
4. Aron is a chef who works at a restaurant that's called Prima.
5. Tuffy is one of Amy's cats that used to be very shy when Amy first adopted it.

B. **2.** who is jealous of Nick
3. who's wearing the blue sweater
4. who work in the news division at *Newsline*
5. Sample answer: *Big Fish*; that's about a guy who visits his father before he dies
6. Sample answer: lacrosse; sport that's played on an outdoor field with sticks that have nets on the end

Language Functions

Sample answers:
1. Please don't interrupt me.
2. You may be right.
3. you're wrong about that
4. Will you let me finish?
5. I see your point.

Unit B.3

Listening

A. **2.** f   **5.** a   **8.** b
3. h   **6.** e   **9.** g
4. j   **7.** i   **10.** c

B. **1.** combination
2. images; emotions; imagination
3. change
4. influenced

Vocabulary

2. ask him or her out
3. seeing somebody
4. to play hard to get
5. are playing the field
6. split up
7. are on the rebound
8. be in a serious relationship
9. fix you up
10. go on a blind date

Grammar 1

2. will probably feel; ask him out
3. date; split up; will have
4. continue; will find out
5. won't end; isn't
6. observe; will see
7. laughs; makes; will probably agree
8. avoids; checks; doesn't show; won't go out

BONUS
Sample answers:
1. If you go out with someone you work with, you'll have a hard time focusing on your work.
2. If you try calling her up, she might be interested. If you keep following her, she will be frightened.
3. Maybe if you ask her how she feels, she'll be straightforward.

Grammar 2

1. had just come; was
2. had started; had been; was always
3. Had we gotten; went
4. didn't we have; said; had always wanted; think
5. turned; saw
6. had never studied; had
7. we've forgotten; haven't forgotten

Grammar 3

A. **2.** difficult for me to believe
3. pleased to have
4. wrong for us to regret; ready to move
5. anxious to find out

B. **2.** money to leave
3. permission to use
4. ability to pull; potential to become

C. Sample answers:
1. It's not easy for me to speak English on the telephone. I have to have a lot of courage to try.
2. I was really pleased to hear that I did well on my last test. I think I have a lot of potential to become successful!

Language Functions

1. I was just thinking about when we went to France in high school on an exchange program.
2. What a nightmare that was!
3. I should have stayed in touch with him.
4. How could I forget?

Unit B.4

Listening

A. **2.** ~~When I haven't heard from you~~ When I hadn't heard from you
3. ~~I am just going to call you~~ I was just going to call you
4. ~~Jackie said that she poses as a Kicks executive~~ Jackie said that she had posed as a Kicks executive
5. ~~And they both admitted that there is no Kicks!~~ And they both admitted that there was no Kicks!
6. ~~And Dean actually had said that he had sent the tape~~ And Dean actually said that he had sent the tape
7. ~~I just cleaned it~~ I just had it cleaned
8. ~~I'm just about to try that~~ I was just about to try that
9. ~~I was checking it after I sat down~~ I was going to check it after I sat down

B.

Tornado Devastates County	Baby and Dad Doing Well after Liver Surgery	Rock Star Weds in Ireland
left a track of were hit by were injured	is reported to be doing well reported to be in stable condition	all of whom attended one of the original members of from his previous

Vocabulary

2. g **4.** c **6.** e **8.** b **10.** h
3. a **5.** f **7.** i **9.** j

Grammar 1

A. **1.** are you going to do; was going to stay
2. are going to cancel; were going to go; am going to reschedule
3. were going to go out

B. Sample answers:
1. Yesterday I was going to go to bed early, but I talked on the phone to my mother instead.
2. On Monday I was going to eat at a restaurant with some friends, but we decided to order food in instead.

Grammar 2

A. **2.** get it repaired / have it repaired
3. have it serviced / get it serviced
4. had it replaced / got it replaced
5. getting it serviced / having it serviced
6. get it restored / having it restored

B. Sample answers:
1. I had my car washed last week.
2. I'm going to get some shirts dry cleaned tomorrow.
3. I've had my résumé checked by a job search service.

Grammar 3

A. **2.** that the Drama club meeting had just ended; she had been waiting outside for her mom to pick her up
3. Mr. Field told me that he had seen the lockers in the hallway shaking.
4. Cindy noted that all the cars in the street had stopped.
5. Mr. Field stated that he had gotten down on the floor, under his desk.
6. Cindy said that she had run to a nearby building and had stood in a doorway.
7. Mr. Field complained that the next day he was going to have to clean up the mess in the office.
8. Cindy Nakano said that she didn't know. She guessed that the school was probably going to cancel classes that week.

B. Sample answers:
1. My teacher said that he was getting married next month.
2. My friend complained that her roommate is too noisy.

Language Functions

1. Something's wrong with the
2. What we ought to do is
3. Let's give that a try.
4. What are we going to do?!
5. Have you tried checking
6. Why don't we

Unit C.1

Listening

A. **2.** ~~we are supposed to celebrate~~ we were supposed to be celebrating
3. ~~I just wish I was more careful~~ I just wish I had been more careful
4. ~~I hope you'll stop~~ I wish you would stop
5. ~~I'm a professional~~ I'm supposed to be a professional
6. ~~I wish we could go back and do it again~~ I wish I could go back and do it over
7. ~~You just need to forget the past and move on~~ You just have to forget what's done and go on
8. ~~if you didn't do such a good job of covering the story, we never would know the truth~~ if you hadn't done such a good job of covering the story, we never would have known the truth

B. **1.** c **3.** a **5.** h **7.** d **9.** i
2. g **4.** f **6.** b **8.** j **10.** e

BONUS:
1. *Optimist:* 1, 2, 3, 4, 5, 6, 9, (10 = half full)
2. *Pessimist:* 7, 8, (10 = half empty)

Vocabulary

1. oversees
2. overlooked
3. overheard
4. overcharging me
5. overreact
6. overdid it on the salt
7. overestimated
8. overeat

Grammar 1

A. **Josh:**

2. I wish I had complimented her on her outfit.
3. I wish I hadn't said, "You remind me of my mother." / I wish I hadn't said that she reminded me of my mother.
4. I wish the taxi driver would drive faster.

Mandy:

5. I wish Josh hadn't brought me flowers. / I wish I weren't allergic to flowers.
6. I wish Josh had said he liked my outfit.
7. I wish I didn't sound nervous.
8. I wish the taxi driver weren't driving so fast.

BONUS
Sample answer:
Josh: I wish that I hadn't talked so much at dinner. I wish I had listened more to Mandy.

B. Sample answers:

1. I wish my roommate wouldn't be so messy.
2. I wish my friend at home would call me more often.
3. I wish I could paint beautiful pictures.
4. I wish I weren't so shy.
5. I wish I had gone out to dinner when Sam invited me.

Grammar 2

A. 2. If I hadn't eaten too (so) much, I wouldn't have felt sick after dinner.
3. If I hadn't made him feel uncomfortable, he wouldn't have felt sick.
4. If I had worn my best black dress, Josh would have complimented me.

B. Sample answer:
I didn't go to my friend's play. If I hadn't had so much homework, I would have gone. If I'd gone, my friend wouldn't be angry with me.

Grammar 3

1. was supposed to get
2. am supposed to finish
3. isn't supposed to open
4. isn't supposed to be
5. are supposed to look
6. am . . . supposed to make

Language Functions

1. I blew it
2. don't worry about it
3. have let that happen
4. be so hard on yourself
5. feel bad
6. How could she do that?
7. my fault
8. made a terrible mistake
9. worry about it
10. nothing we can do about it now

Listening

A. 1. I certainly do.   4. small condition
      2. great story   5. not to press
      3. will make us   6. I'll tell

B. 1. invited   5. recorded
      2. didn't really have   6. took over
      3. met   7. promised to introduce
      4. took   8. found out

C. 1. C   3. I   5. I   7. I
      2. I   4. C   6. I   8. C

Vocabulary

1. come forward   5. come through
2. came out   6. came across
3. come between   7. comes up
4. came down with

Grammar 1

A. 2. could help; didn't have
      3. installed; would have
      4. prepared; wouldn't need; 'd be
      5. included; would watch; would encourage
      6. offered; would exercise; wouldn't cost; would feel; felt; would perform

B. Sample answers:
1. If my apartment had more space, it would be more comfortable. If I had more money, I would get a better apartment. If I moved the furniture around, maybe the apartment would feel more spacious.
2. If I got more sleep at night, I would have more energy during the day. If I had more energy, I would probably work more efficiently.

Grammar 2

1. had you been taking
2. hadn't; hadn't been; been
3. had been struggling
4. I'd been taking; appeared
5. had been dreaming
6. played; had been studying
7. Did Dean come up with; he did
8. did; had been living; didn't want
9. saved; hadn't been getting; started receiving

Grammar 3

A. 2. You shouldn't have worn
      3. you shouldn't have gone
      4. I should have brought
      5. You shouldn't have reported
      6. I / We should have ordered

B. 2. A   3. R   4. R   5. B   6. R

C. Sample dialogs:
   1. **Your friend:** I don't feel well at all.
      You: You shouldn't have eaten so much!
   2. **Your classmate:** Do you want to go to the movies tonight?
      You: I do want to, but I can't. I should have written my paper last night. I shouldn't have waited! Now I have to work tonight.

Language Functions

1. I can't wait. / It's going to be great. / I'm really looking forward to it. / I'm so excited about it.
2. I'm not too thrilled about it. / I'm not too excited about it. / I wish I didn't have to work. / Actually, I really don't want to.
3. I bet. / I can imagine. / I know what you mean. / I can understand that. / I don't blame you.
4. I'm kind of worried about her.
5. I bet. / I can imagine. / I would be, too. / I know what you mean. / I can understand that. / I don't blame you.
6. I'm not really up for it. / I couldn't care less about it.

Unit C.3

Listening

A.
2. Dean	**b.** 10
3. Dean	**c.** 11
4. Nick	**d.** 9
5. Jackie	**e.** 5
6. Jackie	**f.** 1
7. Nick	**g.** 7
8. Nick	**h.** 8
9. Dean	**i.** 3
10. Coach	**j.** 12
11. Nick	**k.** 4
12. Nick	**l.** 2

B. 2. e   3. a   4. d   5. b

C.
2. it ended differently
3. I start to feel lost
4. out of the corner of my eye
5. heart beating fast
6. wide, empty stage
7. waiting for me to perform
8. red velvet cape
9. this beautiful song
10. starts applauding
11. shaking hands with everyone
12. looking into my eyes
13. pat it on the head

Vocabulary

1. loud	5. smooth
2. eye	6. soft
3. hot; fit	7. looks; thin
4. warm	8. tired

Grammar 1

A.
2. will be doing interviews for 5 national talk shows. Everyone in the country will know who she is.
3. will be sunbathing on a beautiful beach. They'll be sipping cold lemonade.
4. will be thinking about her new position as a reporter at *Newsline*.
5. will be reviewing resumes from background researchers who will want Talia's old job.
6. . . . Nick will be practicing with the soccer team. His teammates will be happy for him.
7. . . . . Nick will be thinking about Talia and will wonder if he should call her.
8. . . . Nick will be discussing an endorsement deal from "Steps," a real athletic shoe company.

B. Sample answers:
1. On Tuesday, I'm going to be studying hard, because there's a test on Wednesday.
2. On Wednesday, I'm going to be relaxing in the evening!
3. On the weekend, I'm going to be walking in the park, if the weather is nice.

Grammar 2

2. ~~that I picked it up~~ that I picked up
3. ~~which I had seen earlier~~ whom I had seen earlier; ~~a kind king had given it to me~~ that a kind king had given me
4. ~~whom the bird had dropped it~~ that the bird had dropped
5. ~~I had brushed them so carefully for years~~ which I had brushed so carefully for years
6. ~~that you have been experiencing it~~ that you have been experiencing; ~~who you are having right now~~ that you are having right now
7. ~~about that you dreamed~~ that you dreamed about; ~~that is it painted~~ that it is painted
8. ~~that was being eaten it~~ that you were eating
9. ~~whom you lost~~ that you lost

Grammar 3

2. We can't be beaten / beat with you on the team.
3. The interview has to be recorded on video.
4. The story can't be aired without Talia's interview.
5. The meeting can be rescheduled for tomorrow morning.
6. Coach Haskins ought to be told first.

Language Functions

1. believe that
2. That really burns
3. get so upset
4. How dare he
5. an outrage
6. won't do any good
7. ticks me off

Unit C.4

Listening

A. 1. she's been offered
2. she's been working
3. haven't had a chance

B. 1. spend more time
2. turned (*Newsbeat*) down
3. made a fool
4. like most

C. 1. d 3. g 5. e 7. f
2. a 4. b 6. h 8. c

Vocabulary

1. break the ice
2. break the news
3. break her heart
4. break the record
5. break the habit
6. broken new ground
7. break my promise
8. break a law

Grammar 1

A. 3. It was just yesterday that I started using Glitter.
4. A friend of mine who has beautiful teeth recommended Glitter to me.
5. Glitter is the only brand that can give you the white, bright smile that you've always dreamed of.
6. Can you tell me the name of the store where you bought Glitter?
7. The only way to get the toothpaste that will change your life is to visit our website— glittertoothpaste.com.

B. Sample answer:
I like the bag that my friend gave me on my birthday. The bag has a lot of pockets where I can keep my pens, cell phone, and portable CD player. The bag is a really cool color that I like a lot.

Grammar 2

A. 2. do; do; did
3. does
4. do; do
5. did
6. WILL
7. WOULD

B. Sample dialog:
Your friend: I really liked the movie *Cold Mountain*. It's such a beautiful story of a wartime romance. And the scenery was gorgeous!
You: Well, the scenery WAS gorgeous, but I thought that the story was not beautiful at all. I found it really boring!
Your friend: But Renee Zellweger was so amazing! Her character had a lot of strength.
You: Yes, I agree, her character did have a lot of strength. And Renee Zellweger's acting IS really good.

Grammar 3

2. go along with it
3. fix me up
4. think of my work
5. worked out for them
6. comes between them
7. turn out for it
8. put it off
9. think it over
10. get along with her
11. lets them down
12. count on her

Language Functions

1. meaning / planning / wanting
2. plan to do
3. work out well for you
4. keep coming up
5. you planning to do / your plans
6. Keep me posted / Let me know what happens / Let me know how things turn out / Let me know how everything goes / Keep in touch.